THE RESTAURANT
BOOK

THE DEFINITIVE GUIDE TO
STARTING YOUR OWN RESTAURANT

THE RESTAURANT BOOK

RICHARD WARE & JAMES RUDNICK

FACTS ON FILE PUBLICATIONS
NEW YORK, NEW YORK • OXFORD, ENGLAND

Acknowledgements

The authors wish to express their appreciation to Robert McClelland, an acclaimed Toronto consultant, and John Marshall, a leading food-service designer, for the help they offered during the writing of this book.

Library of Congress Cataloging-in-Publication Data

Ware, Richard.
  The restaurant book.

  Includes index.
  1. Restaurant management.   I. Rudnick, James.
II. Title.
TX911.3.M27W37   1986   647'.95'068   85-25206
ISBN 0-8160-2091-4

Printed in the United States

10 9 8 7 6 5 4 3 2 1

CONTENTS

FOREWORD

As consultants to the restaurant industry, we are constantly being asked: "How can I start up my own restaurant? And which books do you recommend on the subject?"

In researching these questions, we found that there are no books available for the budding restaurateur. So we decided to pool thirty-five years of experience and write a book that would serve as a guide for anyone wishing to enter the restaurant business.

By following the book's chapter-by-chapter guidelines, you will reach an understanding of the process involved in opening a restaurant. And by the end of this book, you will have all the information necessary to decide whether or not you want to become involved in the restaurant industry.

This book will be not only your first, but by far the best and cheapest investment you can make to help fulfill your restaurant dream.

Richard Ware
James Rudnick

THE RESTAURANT
BOOK

1

THE MYTHS & REALITIES

You might think that opening a new restaurant is an easy task. Such thinking may account for the reason that so many people try to turn their dreams into reality every year. But dreams can become reality only for those who are willing to acknowledge that along with reality comes hard work! It takes hard work not only to run the new restaurant, but also to plan a successful new venture. The steps in planning a new restaurant are varied, and all are essential to success. In the following chapters, we will outline these steps and attempt to guide you along the way.

The National Restaurant Association keeps no statistics but the New York State Restaurant Association reports that in their state 75 percent of all restaurants fail or change hands within five years of opening. Thus, many dreams are shattered, perhaps because prospective restaurateurs are uninformed about what they are getting themselves into. Many hear and believe only the myths about the restaurant industry. Somehow, the realities of the business remain unexplained or ignored.

It is pleasant to be your own boss and to see a dream become reality while you are making money. But make no mistake! Remember that above all, the life of a restaurateur involves work coupled with responsibility; to forget this fact is to court disaster.

Case Study—The Restaurateur and the Insurance Agent

"Richard? Richard, is that you?"

Richard Brown turned around slowly. This cocktail party is damn crowded, he thought. Now just who is this guy? "Uh, yes.

It's Richard Brown. Say, listen, I'm sorry but these high school reunions are murder. I remember the face, but . . ."

"Jim. Jim Green. That's okay. It's been about ten or eleven years, right?"

Richard took another sip of his lukewarm drink and nodded.

"Listen, Richard, I'm into insurance and we've got a great new policy just coming into force. You might think that . . ."

"Uh, no thanks, Jim. I have all the insurance I need right now." Richard said, edging away.

Jim laid a hand on Richard's retreating sleeve. "Well sure, no problem, Richard. What are you into, anyway?"

"Actually," Richard said, "I own a restaurant here in town."

"Oh, a restaurant, eh? Sounds like you've got it made! Just one big continuous party, eh?"

"Well, actually Jim, it's not quite . . ."

"And being the boss, you come in whenever you like, too!"

"The hours are really very . . ."

"And imagine. Going up to the bar and having a drink anytime, and paying yourself for doing it, too!"

"Really, Jim, that's something you try to avoid. There just isn't . . ."

"And having all your friends pay to come and see you. You can get them a table just like that, without waiting either!"

Richard shook his head. "To be fair about things, you should . . ."

Jim rambled on, not even hearing Richard. ". . . and always taking home the best steaks and lobsters."

"Normally, it's left-overs, Jim. That other stuff is too expensive . . ."

"On top of all that money coming in, the write-offs are great. Your car, the house, the furniture, your wife's salary."

"You've got to make it first before you can . . ."

"All those nights out, you probably write them off too, as research into the competition or something. And all those women around. Boy, I can just imagine!"

"I am married, you know. And after awhile you . . ."

"Boy, sure sounds like the life to me. And here I am just selling insurance. Did I pick wrong! Maybe I should get into the restaurant business, too. What do you think, Richard?"

Richard moved away, pausing only to answer his old school mate. "Sounds like you've got it all covered, Jim. Good luck and good-bye!"

The Realities

The first step in analyzing what the life of a restaurateur is really like is to dispel all those myths that have been built up over the years.

1. *Party all the time!* No, it's work, hard work most of the time.
2. *Your hours are your own!* That's true, all 70 to 100 per week.
3. *Drink anytime for free!* Well, you can hardly run a business if you are never sober, and it's your own profits that you'll be drinking.
4. *Eat what you like!* Again, it's your money, and you will soon find that eating twice or three times a day in the same restaurant, even if it is your own, produces boredom.
5. *Get a table for friends or relatives anytime they drop in!* Sure, and they might expect you to pick up the check, too. Also what will other customers think if they have to wait longer for a table?
6. *Write anything and everything off as expenses!* You have to make the money before you can spend it.
7. *Deduct evenings out as research!* If you do have an evening off, the last thing you will probably want to do is visit someone else's restaurant.
8. *Make lots of money!* Well, we hope you will, but not everyone does.
9. *Be your own boss!* For this privilege, you have to make all the decisions.

Qualities Necessary to be a Restaurateur

The life of the restaurateur is very different from that of most other professionals and, therefore, difficult to fully characterize. Because of the demands made on those of us in the business, we've learned many things to help us cope. Some of the necessary qualities we brought with us; others we picked up along the way. Here is a partial list of them.

Physical Qualities

Strong Back — You are frequently lifting things and putting heavy cases into storage.

Strong Legs — You are standing and walking all day long.

Healthy Feet — You are on your feet all day and all night long.

Need Little Sleep — You often spend seventy to one hundred hours in your restaurant. You are up early and to bed late; you need to be able to get by on little sleep.

Healthy Stomach — You seldom get a chance to sit down and eat at regular mealtimes because of customer demands.

Skills

Buyer — You have to be willing to negotiate for prices and terms with all your suppliers.

Receiver — You must be able to receive your goods, weigh them in, and know if they are within your specifications.

Plumber — You should be able to fix all the small leaks and deal with the floods. Plumbers mean money.

Electrician — You should be able to fix your circuits when they blow and know, when something breaks down, why it did.

Mr. Fixit — When there is an equipment breakdown, you should be able to make the necessary repairs to enable your operations to continue, even if only temporarily. You should know why your cash register went off, how to fix it, and how to read all tapes.

Carpenter & Painter — You should be able to fix all your woodwork so that it can be used, and paint or stain surfaces where necessary.

Diplomat — You must be able to handle all customer complaints.

Math Wizard — You must be able to balance your cash, deposits, tills, inventory, accounts, payroll, and taxes, and deal with all other financial matters.

Bank Expert	You must be able to approach your lender with a plan of repayment and deal with him or her on a long-term basis.
Credit Expert	You must be able to drive a good bargain on your own terms with suppliers, and scrutinize your major equipment suppliers on their terms as well.
Manager	You must be able to train your staff thoroughly on the correct procedures.
Babysitter	You must like children; they are everywhere in this business.
People Person	Because they too are everywhere, you must really enjoy dealing with people all the time.
Business Person	Because it is a business, you are in it to make a profit.

To see if your goals change as you read this book, ask yourself these questions now and then again when you reach the end:

1. What type of restaurant do I see myself owning?
2. How much will it cost me to get into the business?
3. How much money do I think I will make?

By answering these questions at the beginning and at the end of the book and comparing the results, you will see how many myths were dispelled and how beneficial this book has been to you.

Many people feel that because they eat in restaurants several times a month, they understand just about everything they need to know. By comparison, we all drive cars, but how many of us truly understand what goes on under the hood? Very few!

2

CHEESEBURGERS TO CHATEAUBRIAND

For many people, the environment in which they work is as important as the job they are performing. Fitting in with our fellow workers and being comfortable in our surroundings are two important factors in job satisfaction for many of us.

Going into business for one's self is no different in this respect. We must like the life-style, the environment, and the people we employ, because we are going to spend a large part of our day in these surroundings.

Case Study—Square Pegs in Round Holes

Herb Bell didn't really mind his job. All day long he sat behind his desk and processed invoices for a new-car dealership. He barely saw his secretary each day, just paperwork by the pile. He'd gotten used to it over the fourteen years he'd had this job: coffee at 10:15, lunch promptly at 12:00, and coffee again at 3:00. He enjoyed the routine, when he bothered to think about it.

Then his lawyer called to inform him that he had inherited almost $50,000. He was stunned for a few weeks. Each day, he went to work, but the thought of that money sitting there created a pressure he was not used to. I think I'll go into business, thought Herb. The restaurant business. And so he did.

He researched the business as well as he could, and discovered that a franchised fast-food outlet would be within his price range. A franchised operation had at least some potential for success, he reasoned, or else franchises wouldn't be sold.

On opening day, Herb figured he'd gotten lucky. The hamburger franchise he had picked was a big one, and he was busy right off the bat. But somehow he never got used to the big rush of customers that started to flood in just before noon. There were production schedules to begin almost every hour, given his volume of business, and he seemed to get flustered whenever a crisis arose.

All his staff were young, inexperienced part-time students, and Herb realized that he had trouble motivating them. But what really bothered him was the screaming of the children. They were everywhere, yelling and running, gathering in groups all over the restaurant, laughing and screeching while he had to be on his feet all day long. Herb was miserable. After only three months of being in business he realized he was not happy. Sales were good, but now he hated his job. He needed a change.

Herb was lucky. A few months later, he was able to sell out and recoup his investment. However, as he looked around, he realized he'd given up a good job with fourteen years of seniority. He still had his money in the bank, but now what?

Case Study Analysis

Herb really was a square peg in a round hole. It's a pity he didn't realize what enormous changes in his life-style he would encounter. Perhaps if he had asked himself the following questions, he wouldn't have made the move:

1. Do I like the hustle and bustle of meeting deadlines every day, or do I like moving at my own pace?
2. Do I like the challenge of solving problems instantly, or do I prefer to put them on the back burner until later?
3. Can I stand on my feet all day, or do I tire easily?
4. Do I enjoy motivating young untrained staff, or do I prefer to deal only with experienced employees?
5. Do I feel comfortable around children, or can I take them only in moderation?

What Kind of Restaurant Should You Be In?

In order to seriously consider entering the restaurant business, you must have a fairly good idea about what type of restaurant is best for you. As we've seen in the case study, many people just don't realize how enormous the change in their life-style will be when they are running a restaurant.

It's a difficult decision at best, because there are so many different types of restaurants. We can see them on almost every corner in every neighborhood. However, the confusion lessens when it is realized that most restaurants can be classified as one of several types. We will compare the types by looking at their similarities and differences. Probably, the examples will be familiar to you, but remember, there are always exceptions to any such grouping.

Some restaurants may be licensed, others unlicensed, as noted below. This "license" refers to a Liquor License, the rights granted by your state to serve liquor, wine or beer to the public, to your customers.

Fast-Food

A fast-food restaurant is one that sells quickly prepared foods. This kind of restaurant is often a franchise operation. The limited menu is generally low- to medium-priced; the food is mainly take-out in disposable containers. Residential areas provide the high volume needed by the fast-food chains located in free-standing buildings. Strip plazas and malls also provide traffic for volume sales. Help required is minimal and need not be highly trained. Seating is limited. Investment varies according to the type of franchise purchased. The franchisor usually specifies decor, menu, type and quality of food, suppliers, equipment, and prices.

Local Small Restaurant

Short orders, quick service, and fast turnover best characterize this style. The investment is not high, as decor is usually minimal. Not many comforts are offered to customers. Seating is limited to counters and a few tables and booths. Employees are not highly trained. The right location in high-density population areas, such as office buildings, is the key for the high customer counts necessary. However, rent can be high. Menu is usually very extensive and varied, with low to medium prices. A large portion of the business is take-out at coffee break and lunchtime.

Family Style (licensed or unlicensed)

A large menu with medium pricing is generally offered by family restaurants. Investment can be high because of the decor and seating in these generally large and brightly decorated restaurants. Plenty of parking must be provided. Employees are usually well trained in dealing with large family groups. A reputation for value and good service will result in repeat business.

Dinnerhouse (licensed)
Generally, these free-standing buildings are located near easy-access, high-traffic roadways. Their casual, licensed dining rooms provide an easy, fun-style atmosphere. These operations are usually very systematized and controlled, and are often part of a large chain operation. Employees are usually well trained and provide good casual service. Investment here is usually very large. Many dinnerhouses are of the "theme" nature, with themes running through design, layout, decor, staff, and menu.

Ethnic
The ethnic restaurant has a menu based on the cooking of one country. Decor is usually appropriate to this theme. Authenticity in food and service is usually very important to the customer. These restaurants can range in style from fast-food to gourmet. Staff is well trained and very knowledgeable about their menu. Investment is often high because of the authentic decor.

Pub-Bar Style
Although these restaurants feature a limited menu, they are generally promoted as meeting places. The singles' bar restaurant is designed with a large stand-up bar to encourage the customer to mingle with others. Often trendy, these restaurants can be located almost anywhere, but their life span may be limited as customers move on to visit more current places.

Gourmet
Small and intimate surroundings provide an appropriate atmosphere for the expensive and specialized meals. This kind of restaurant concentrates on promoting high standards and establishing a reputation which draws customers back time and time again. The chef and staff are highly trained, and are noted for giving personalized service. Investment is usually high. Less frequent turnover is needed because of the high guest-check averages. Location can be almost anywhere, as customers will search out this type of restaurant.

As an owner, you will be spending many hours in your new restaurant, and these hours will be spent working, not relaxing with your customers. So the kind of restaurant you choose to open should be appropriate, not only to your pocket book, but to your life-style as well.

What It Will Cost

You may be the exception and wish to build your own restaurant, but as a rule, most first-time operators will lease their premises. The premises they lease can be anything from a standard shopping mall shell to an old barn, and anything in between.

Because of the wide range of options and the vast differences in costs in various parts of the United States, it is very difficult to say specifically what it will cost you to finish off your particular restaurant, but we can give you some general guidelines to take into account when thinking about price.

What follows are descriptions of three different kinds of operations that illustrate the costs involved in constructing and equipping a foodservice facility from scratch.

Fast-Food Outlet
Our first example is a fast-food hamburger outlet situated in a shopping mall, approximately 500 square feet in size.

a. Construction
There are no costs involved here, as the landlord built the shopping mall and is leasing the premises to the tenants for their specific requirements.

b. Leasehold Improvements
This section includes the costs of perparing plans and drawings, obtaining all the necessary permits, connecting exhaust ducts, air conditioning, water, power and drainage to the landlord's services, erection of all partition walls, finishes to walls, floors and ceiling, and all labor and supervision. The costs will depend on the quality of the materials used, but will run in the range of $160 to $190 per square foot, for a total cost of between $80,000 and $95,000.

c. Equipment
The cost of purchasing all cooking and service equipment (broiler, fryers, refrigerator, freezer, and display cases), the necessary stainless steel fabrication (for sinks, counters and shelving), and the cash register, menu boards, and signage would be in the area of $37,500.

d. Furnishings
There are no purchases required here as the landlord is providing a fully furnished common-seating area. However, the landlord requires a $10,000 capital cost contribution from each of the fast-food tenants to offset the cost of this area.

As you can see, the total cost of our hamburger outlet is between $127,500 and $142,500. If we were constructing a different kind of outlet, such as a delicatessen that did not require exhaust ventilation or heavy electrical power or a gas supply, then the cost of our leasehold improvements and even our equipment requirements would be drastically reduced.

Free-Standing Dinnerhouse
Our dinnerhouse example is situated on a main thoroughfare, and is approximately 5,000 square feet in size, with 250 seats including the bar area.

a. Construction
The dinnerhouse operator found an ideal location on which the landlord was offering to build "to suit" any prospective tenant, on a lease-back basis with a twenty-year lease.

b. Leasehold Improvements
This includes the cost of all interior and exterior finishes: plans, permits, mechanical, electrical, plumbing, carpentry, and all interior partitions and finishes.

Again, the actual cost will vary according to the quality of materials used and how detailed the decor is, but will be in the $80 to $100 per square foot range, totaling $400,000 to $500,000.

c. Equipment
The equipment package can be broken down into three areas:

1. Kitchen equipment, including all cooking and storage equipment, stainless steel fabrication, sinks, counters, and dishwashers will cost in the region of $120,000 to $130,000.
2. Smallwares, which will include all cutlery, dishware, glasses and table accompaniments, will be in the $12,500 to $17,500 range.
3. Systems can vary greatly depending on your requirements, and the detail and control you require. This area will include a liquor control system costing $7,200, cash control system costing $17,500, and a sound system costing $6,500, for a total of $31,200.

d. Furnishings
This again is an area that can vary greatly, depending on the quality and requirements. But a good rule of thumb would be a cost of $175 per seat, which includes all chairs, stools and tables, giving a total cost on our 250-seat operation of $43,750.

As you can see, costs can vary depending on menu requirements, type of decor used, and quality of the equipment and furnishings you purchase. In our example, the cost ranges between $607,450 and $722,450, or approximately $2,430 to $2,890 per restaurant seat. It can be done for less, but also for a lot more.

Speciality Ethnic Restaurant
We will use as our example an Italian restaurant situated on a commercial city street with other retail operations on either side. The total space is 3,000 square feet with 150 seats.

a. Construction
The property is leased. Because of the improvements our tenant will have to make to the landlord's property, the landlord is giving the tenant a $5 per square foot allowance, giving the tenant $15,000.

b. Leasehold Improvements
The cost of all interior and, in this case, only minimal exterior finishes (street frontage) includes the same factors as our previous example. Although we are dealing with a smaller space, the same type and amount of work is involved, with only a slight saving on

materials. The cost would be in the $80 to $90 per square foot range, totaling $240,000 to $270,000.

c. Equipment
This cost again would be only marginally smaller than our previous example, as the requirements remain the same:

1. Kitchen equipment would cost approximately $100,000.
2. Smallwares, with fewer place settings required, would be about $90,000.
3. Systems in this case would include a fairly inexpensive sound system at $3,000, a single-department cash register at $3,000, but no automated pouring and inventory controlled bar system. Total cost $6,000.

d. Furnishings
Again, using our $175 per seat guideline, these would cost $26,250. Therefore, our Italian-style operation would cost in the area of $462,250 to $492,250 or between $3,082 and $3,282 per restaurant seat. Not much difference from our previous example, calculated on a per-seat basis.

Other Start-Up Costs

Even though we have tried to give you some idea of the actual costs involved in starting an operation, you will find that there are many other start-up costs that are not apparent to the beginner but which, nevertheless, have to be considered. It is impossible for us to put a dollar figure against any of the items on the following list; however, the subsequent chapters in this book will tell you either how to arrive at a cost for each area or how to find out the information;

1. Legal Fees
2. Accounting Fees and Costs
3. Research and Development
4. Printing and Graphics
5. Travel Expenses
6. Consulting Fees
7. General and Office
8. Uniforms
9. Pre-Opening Salaries
10. Inventory
11. Initial Advertising
12. Cash Floats
13. Pre-Opening Utilities and Telephone
14. Insurance
15. Pre-Opening Rent
16. Pest Control
17. Allowance for Cost Over-Runs
18. Working Capital

3

TAKING THE FIRST STEPS

Every business idea has to start with a product or service. In the restaurant business you must start with the menu; this is the essential ingredient. Once you have decided upon the product you are going to be offering and have formulated your menu, you can start to answer a number of other questions:

1. What will the theme or concept be?
2. What name should you give your restaurant?
3. What kind of service will you provide?
4. What kind of seating will you require?
5. What will your food and labor costs be?
6. Where should you locate?
7. What equipment will you require?
8. What kind of customer will you appeal to?
9. Who will supply the products that you require?

The Menu

The menu is your first step. But how do you decide what the main item or items on your menu should be? Well, you may already have this questioned answered. If your reason for going into the restaurant business is that you have a great recipe for corned beef and cabbage, then you have already decided on your main menu item. But you will still have to consider how popular your great recipe will be with the general public.

If you are undecided as to what your restaurant should offer, then consider the following points:

1. What do you personally feel most comfortable with? You would not consider opening a fish and chip store if you have an allergy to fish products.
2. What do you know the most about? The more background knowledge you have regarding a certain product, the more understanding and appreciation you will have in preparing and cooking the item.
3. What item is either lacking in your area or not being done well? Be sure that you really can do better.
4. What are the trends within the restaurant industry? Are these trends just fads, or will they receive long-term recognition?

Therefore, the items that you choose to feature on your menu may depend on a number of factors. It is up to you to decide what is best for you and your particular area.

Menu Pricing

Knowing what to charge for each menu item is one of the most difficult tasks you will face if you are a new restaurateur. Your pricing has to be competitive, and yet you must still ensure a profit at the end of the day. Pricing can depend on volume. Compared with other hamburger outlets, McDonald's food costs may be quite high, but they can rely on a high volume of customers to sustain a profit. If you serve 100 customers and make 10¢ on each one, or you serve 10 customers and make $1 on each one, you will make the same profit. But you have to know these figures in order to prepare your sales projections (see Chapter 4) and to know what price to affix to each menu item.

If, after ascertaining all your other costs, you decide you have to maintain a food cost of 35 percent to make a profit, then there are certain factors you will have to weigh.

1. Certain items may be priced too high if you wish to maintain an overall cost of 35 percent; on the other hand, some items may be priced too low. It may be necessary to price items according to what you feel the customer will accept. This policy may mean pricing one item at a 25 percent food cost and another at a 45 percent food cost. You have to determine what the selling mix of these items will be in order to arrive at an overall food cost of 35 percent.

2. Don't forget that the cost of an item is often more than you realize. An order of fish and chips may seem to cost out as follows: one 2 oz. piece of cod @ 50¢ and a serving of chips @ 20¢—total cost 70¢. At a 35 percent food cost, your selling price would be $2. But what about the additional food costs involved in serving this product, such as the batter in which you dip your fish, the oil in which you fry both the fish and the chips, the lemon wedge that you put on each serving, the tartar sauce which some customers may request, or the ketchup, vinegar, salt, and pepper? Suddenly the cost of your order of fish and chips has risen to $1. If you are only charging $2, your food cost has risen to 50 percent, and you are on your way out of the restaurant business.

3. Pricing menu items and even the size of portions may have to vary at different service times. If you are situated in a downtown or an industrial area where you cater to a large lunch-time trade, your menu should accommodate the pocket book as well as the appetite of the lunch-time eater. It is also worth remembering that these midday diners are also limited by time, so your menu items should allow you to provide fast service.

The Sales Catalogue

When it comes to the design and printing of their menu, many restaurateurs miss the boat. They seem quite content just to list the items in a bland format, without trying to either entice or entertain the reader. Let us consider the time and expense put into a catalogue by a mail-order company. They could merely list the items they have for sale and save a lot of money, but they know that by putting in a picture and accompanying it with glowing write-ups, they are going to sell a lot more items. If you treat your menu the same way, the end result will be the same. This can be achieved by colored menu-panels for the fast-food take-out location, or by imaginative graphics and wording on printed menus (*see* Sample #1).

Regulations Governing Menus

There are certain regulations governing the printing of menus, which vary from *state to state*. These regulations may require that the menu: state the minimum amount of alcohol that is served in each drink, inform the customer whether or not sales tax is included or is extra, acknowledge the use of other companies' trade names or trademarks, and adhere to the truth in advertising. This last point means you can't advertise that you are serving one thing, and actually substitute another. This is not only illegal but it could prove very harmful to your customers. Imagine that a customer has an allergy to animal fats, and you advertise in your menu that your french fries are only fried in peanut oil, when, in fact, you are frying them in beef fat to save money. The net result could be very costly, in terms of lost customers and possible legal action.

The Concept

Choosing the right concept for your restaurant is the next important step in fulfilling your restaurant dream. You may have decided that your operation is going to sell pizza as its main item. But your decision to use a 1930's theme or to add Italian decor may make the difference between your restaurant and the others. Your concept or theme may be something typical of your area with which local customers can identify; it may be something that appeals to children if you are going to open a family restaurant; or it could be something trendy, if you are trying to attract the singles market. Your theme can be carried through as far as your finances will allow, or as far as you think is necessary to attract customers. The menu, the type of furniture, the interior decor, the exterior finishes, staff uniforms, and even the style of serving dishes or tableware are all areas that can be used to carry your theme through to its fullest extent. But don't get too carried away; the concept should only be an added attraction to good food and service, never a substitute.

Case Study—Concept Development

Jack James and Bob Roberts had been toying with the idea of opening their own restaurant for some time and had already decided on the kind of operation they wanted: a full-service, licensed pizza and Italian food restaurant that would offer a casual, friendly atmosphere and appeal to patrons of all ages.

SAMPLE #1
CREATIVE MENU DESCRIPTIONS

Aroma	Fresh(ly)	Piled-High
Assorted	Full	Piping-Hot
Baked	Garden Fresh	Refreshing(ly)
Best	Garnished	Rich(ly)
Big	Generous(ly)	Sautéed
Blend	Giant	Seasoned
Broiled	Golden-Brown	Secret(ly)
Carefully	Great	Selection
Char-broiled	Grilled	Selected
Chilled	Heap(ed)(ing)	Sensational
Choice	Hearty	Simmered
Chunky	Homemade	Simmering
Classical	Hot	Sizzling
Colorful	Huge	Smothered
Cool	Iced	Soft
Covered	In Season	Special(ly)
Crisp	Inch-Thick	Spicy
Crunchy	Irresistible(ly)	Stacked
Crusty		Stimulating(ly)
Customized	Juicy	Stuffed
Delectable	Large	Succulent(ly)
Delicate(ly)	Layers	Super
Delicious(ly)	Legendary	Tangy
Delight(ful)(ly)	Light	Tender(ly)
Deluxe	Lightly Breaded	Thick(ly)
Designed	Lightly Seasoned	Thinly
Enjoy	Loaded	Topped
Exotic	Lovingly	Treat
Extra	Meaty	Tropical
Famous	Mouth-Watering	Wrapped
Favorite	Natural	Yummy
Fancy	New	Zesty
Filled	Old-Fashioned	100 percent
Finest	Original	
Flavor(ful)	Perfect(ion)	
Fluffy		

Their main concern was how to make their restaurant different from other similar operations. In fact, their concern was how to develop a unique concept. They decided that the only way they could develop their own theme was to visit every similar restaurant within a twenty-mile radius from where their proposed restaurant was to be located. They split the area in two and agreed to meet in two weeks with their separate findings to see what ideas they could come up with.

At their meeting two weeks later, they discussed the differences between the restaurants they had visited and listed the unique points of each one. Jack had been particularly impressed with one restaurant where they had a life-size model of a Roman centurion in full period costume in the foyer. Once he mentioned this to Bob, the ideas started to flow back and forth. Bob suggested dressing all the staff in Roman costumes; Jack then thought of all the menu ideas they could come up with using the names of famous Romans. They then discussed the possibility of incorporating decor and furnishings that would fit the period.

Six months later, Jack and Bob opened The Roman Centurion, a 150-seat licensed restaurant specializing in Italian cuisine. All the front-of-the-house staff—servers, bar staff, and hostesses—were dressed in either togas or centurion costumes. The menu offered such delights as Nero's Flaming Pizza, and Julius' Caesar Salad, and the interior of the restaurant featured white pillars with lots of black-and-white renderings of historic events and battles.

The seating varied from marble benches with cushions to chariots remade as booths. The salad bar resembled the throne that carried Cleopatra to Rome. Jack and Bob also organized a monthly costume-party night, at which they offered a prize to the customer in the best period dress.

The two owners had created a unique restaurant that was the talk of the area and that was achieving a steady growth in popularity.

Picking a Name

The name you choose for your restaurant is very important, and there are two major things to consider:

1. *Does the name fit your menu?* If you saw a restaurant called the "Jolly Fisherman," you would expect it to sell seafood and not pizza.
2. *Will the name draw the kind of customers that you want?* If your restaurant is geared to the young singles market, with a stand-up bar and chicken wings on the menu, and you called it "La Gondola," two things would probably happen: (a) None of the young singles would frequent your operation, thinking it was a "fine dining" restaurant; (b) The couples market and older clientele would come expecting fine dining, and leave disappointed because they did not get what they had expected.

Your name can also be a great selling feature if you include your main menu item in it, e.g., "Stanley's Fish & Chips." If you have a good product, the name "Stanley" will soon become synonymous in your area with fish and chips.

You can also use a name that will attract immediate attention: "The Hamburger Strikes Back," "Pizza Wars," "Raiders of the Lost Perogi."

They may sound funny, but they will attract attention and probably gain you some free advertising.

Customer Profile

When considering menu, concept, and the name of your restaurant, you must at all times keep in mind your customer profile. In other words, you have to form a mental picture of the kind of people that you want to frequent your establishment. Will they be young singles, or older singles, the twenty-five to forty-year-old couples with families, or the over-forties? Will they be office workers, blue-collar workers, housewives, students, people with money, or those on fixed incomes? Will the restaurant be situated in a rural area, in the downtown core, in the suburbs, or in a shopping mall or plaza? By answering these questions, you will gradually build up a picture or profile of your potential customers. Once you have this profile, it may help you to decide in which direction you should take menu, concept, and name. It will also help you to determine the hours during which your operation will have to be open in order to maximize sales. These same questions also apply when the time comes for choosing a location (*see* Chapter 6).

4

THE BUSINESS PLAN

Defining the Requirements

If you are like most people who go into business, you do not have enough money. So, you have to go shopping. But as on any shopping trip, you have to have a list detailing how much money you need and what you want it for. Your business plan should be professional and accurate. Your accountant can help you greatly in devising your plan. No matter how small the amount or who you are borrowing it from, a well-prepared proposal is essential. It will show that you have put a great deal of thought into your venture and that you are a very professional businessperson.

Outlining your Business

The first step in preparing your business plan is to give as broad an outline as possible of the proposed venture. Remember, the person who will have the final say in approving your loan may have no knowledge of the restaurant business, and the more detailed your outline, the greater the reader's understanding of that outline will be. Here are some of the questions your outline should cover:

1. *Why this particular type of restaurant?* You may have chosen the particular type of restaurant that you propose for many reasons. These may include: (a) Past experience or expertise; (b) To fulfill a particular need in your area; (c) A new or expanding trend in the restaurant industry; (d) Because you feel you can do a better job than similar operations in your area.

All these reasons should be backed up with facts and figures wherever possible. If you can't back them up, then you should question your own reasoning.

2. *Where will the restaurant be located and why?* Again, your reasoning must be sound. Many of the answers to this question will be found in Chapter 6.

3. *Who is the landlord and what are the terms?* At the time of preparing your business plan this information may not be available; if you have already decided on a location, include as much information as you can regarding this aspect. Include a copy of the lease if you have one, or the offer to lease.

4. *When do you plan to open?* The simplest way to answer this question is to prepare a timetable showing the length of time it will take you to open your restaurant from the present time (*see* Sample #2). Once the timetable is prepared, the dates can always be added later, or adjusted as necessary.

5. *Why will your restaurant succeed?* Probably because of many of the factors included above, or a combination of all of them. Remember, it doesn't hurt to blow your own trumpet. If you don't sound confident about your venture, nobody else is going to feel confident either. Whatever the positives, emphasize them: great location, growing area, imaginative concept, original menu theme, high projected sales, low overhead, and so on. The more good reasons you have for success the better, but at all times be honest, or you may only be fooling yourself.

The Start-up Costs

Although many of these costs may be only estimates at this point, always be generous with the amounts. If you think something will cost you $1,000, allow $1,100. By the time you have completed all the work you have to do, prices may well have gone up. (For a list of all the things you have to consider, *see* Sample #3.)

The Operating Projection

The projected statement of operation is the single most important part of your business plan. Your lender and you should be most concerned not with what is on the bottom line, but how you arrived at this figure. Every figure on the projected statement should be backed up with a summary of how you arrived at that figure.

SAMPLE #2
Name of Location
Operational Time-Table

Months	1	2	3	4	5	6	7	8	9	10	11	12
1. Menu Formulation, Fine-Tuning												
2. Concept Development												
3. Investment Proposal												
4. Location Selection												
5. Lease Negotiations												
6. Incorporation of Company												
7. Design & Equipment Specifications												
8. Construction Contract												
9. Equipment & Furnishing Selection												
10. Insurance												
11. Uniform & Product Suppliers												
12. Banking Set-Up												
13. Systems & Accounting Set-Up												
14. Develop Marketing Plan												
15. Set Up Training Program												
16. Hiring												
17. Training & Dry Runs												
18. Opening												

SAMPLE #3
START-UP COSTS

Construction or Renovations
Electrical
Mechanical
Plumbing & Sprinklers
Ceiling & Drywall
Tiling
Concreting
Carpentry Finishes
Interior Finishes
Exterior Finishes
Permits & Insurance
Labor
Supervision
Sundries
    Sub Total:_____

Equipment & Furnishings
Signage
Kitchen Equipment
Restaurant Furnishings
Smallwares
Sound System
Bar System
Cash-Control Systems
    Sub Total:_____

Development Costs
Legal Fees
Accounting Fees
Design Fees
Research & Development
Printing & Graphics
Travel Expenses
Consulting Fees
General & Office
Uniforms
    Sub Total:_____

Pre-Opening Costs
Pre-Opening Salaries
Pre-Opening Inventory
Initial Advertising
Pre-Opening Utilities
Insurance
Cash Float
    Sub Total:_____

Summary

Construction/Renovations   _____
Equipment & Furnishings   _____
Development Costs   _____
Pre-Opening Costs   _____

Sub Total: _____

Contingencies for Cost Overruns   _____

TOTAL   _____

Sample #4 shows a projected operating statement, spread over twelve months. Although your summary of how you arrived at each figure will be based on an annual basis, you should show on your twelve-month spread the seasonal highs and lows in your monthly sales, and consequently any other figures these variations will affect. To ascertain when these highs and lows will occur, you have to have a good understanding of the trading patterns in your area. When researching your location (*see* Chapter 6), other business operators in your area can be very helpful in this respect.

The Average Guest Check

When calculating the potential of any new restaurant, the first critical step is to determine the average guest check. This is simply the average of what each customer will spend in your operation over a given period. For example if you serve 100 customers in a given day, and your sales are $400, your average guest check for that day would be $4—$400 divided by the 100 customers.

Although you may feel, when calculating the average check, that a customer in your restaurant will normally have a hamburger, fries and coffee, totaling $3.00, you have to allow for the customer who just has a coffee, at 40¢. Even if the ratio of hamburgers to coffee customers is 3 to 1, your average guest check is still only $2.35 not $3.00. At 100 customers per day, that's a difference of $65.00, and if you are open 300 days per year, that difference on an annual basis is nearly $20,000. You can now see the importance of arriving at an accurate, average guest check.

Sample #5, The Restaurant Pyramid, details the various types of foodservice outlets and the average guest-check range of each category.

The Sales Forecasting Formula

One of the most important parts of any business plan, especially to lenders, is how much money you've projected you'll make. How do you propose to repay the loan? And will you be able to make a living, so that the loan will be repaid in full? Although sales forecasting is detailed, it is not hard to learn. Here is a breakdown of the steps to take to show the viability of your new restaurant.

SAMPLE #4
Projected Statement of Operation (Mall Location)

	Jan.	Feb.	Mar.	April	May
Sales	23,000	20,000	23,000	25,000	25,000
Cost of Sales	8,050	7,000	8,050	8,750	8,750
Labor Cost	6,000	5,700	6,000	6,000	6,000
Total Cost of Sales	14,050	12,700	14,050	14,750	14,750
Gross Margin	8,950	7,300	8,950	10,250	10,250
OTHER EXPENSES					
Base Rent	1,700	1,700	1,700	1,700	1,700
Percentage Rent	140	(100)	140	300	300
C.A.M./F.A.M.*	520	520	520	520	520
Realty Taxes	310	310	310	310	310
Business Taxes	—	—	—	500	—
Advertising	625	625	625	625	625
Legal & Accounting	—	—	—	—	—
Insurance	700	—	—	—	—
Telephone	35	35	35	35	35
Utilities	330	330	330	330	330
Replacement Cost	—	—	75	—	—
Repairs & Maintenance	100	100	100	100	100
Cleaning Supplies	25	25	25	25	25
Laundry, Linen & Uniforms	40	40	40	40	40
Pest Control	15	15	15	15	15
Drain Cleaning	10	10	10	10	10
General Office & Bookkeeping	100	100	100	100	100
Bank Charges	25	15	15	15	15
Paper Supplies	1,150	1,000	1,150	1,250	1,250
Total Other Expenses	5,825	4,725	5,190	5,875	5,375
Net Profit (Loss)	3,125	2,575	3,760	4,375	4,875
Loan Repayment (P&I)	?	?	?	?	?
Cash Surplus (Deficit)	?	?	?	?	?

* C.A.M.—Common Area Maintenance, usually in a small mall or plaza.
F.A.M.—Food Area Maintenance, usually in a shopping mall.

June	July	Aug.	Sept.	Oct.	Nov.	Dec.	Total	%
24,000	22,000	22,000	25,000	26,000	30,000	35,000	300,000	100
8,400	7,700	7,700	8,750	9,100	10,500	12,250	105,000	35.0
6,000	6,000	6,000	6,000	6,300	7,500	7,500	75,000	25.0
14,400	13,700	13,700	14,750	15,400	18,000	19,750	180,000	60.0
9,600	8,300	8,300	10,250	10,600	12,000	15,250	120,000	40.0
1,700	1,700	1,700	1,700	1,700	1,700	1,700	20,400	6.8
220	60	60	300	380	700	1,100	3,600	1.2
520	520	520	520	520	520	520	6,240	2.1
310	310	310	310	310	310	310	3,720	1.2
500	—	500	—	500	—	—	2,000	0.7
625	625	625	625	625	625	625	7,500	2.5
—	—	—	—	—	—	3,000	3,000	1.0
—	—	—	—	—	—	—	700	0.2
35	35	35	35	35	35	35	420	0.1
330	330	330	330	330	330	330	3,960	1.3
75	—	—	75	—	—	75	300	0.1
100	100	100	100	100	100	100	1,200	0.4
25	25	25	25	25	25	25	300	0.1
310	40	40	40	40	40	40	750	0.2
15	15	15	15	15	15	15	180	0.1
10	10	10	10	10	10	10	120	0.1
100	100	100	100	100	100	100	1,200	0.4
15	15	15	15	15	20	20	200	0.1
1,200	1,100	1,100	1,250	1,300	1,500	1,750	15,000	5.0
6,090	4,985	5,485	5,450	6,005	6,030	9,755	70,790	23.6
3,510	3,315	2,815	4,800	4,595	5,970	5,495	49,210	16.4
?	?	?	?	?	?	?	?	?
?	?	?	?	?	?	?	?	?

The Restaurant Pyramid

Check Average Description Per Person*

Category	Check Average
FINE DINING	$30–$100
HOTELS	$15–$32
DINNERHOUSES	$16–$26
DINNERHOUSES	$8–$14
FAMILY RESTAURANTS	$5–$8
COFFEE SHOPS & CAFETERIAS	$5–$6
FAST FOOD	$4–$5

* including alcoholic beverages (if available), all taxes and tip
Source: Courtesy of Cameron's Foodservice Promotions Reporter

The first step is to establish your projected annual sales for your new restaurant. This is done using the following formula:

SALES = # of seats × turnover × average guest check × operating days.

Number of Seats
Your concept and style of restaurant have already established just how big your restaurant is to be. This number would also include any stand-up-bar room for customers. Layout of the seating would allow for maximum use of space to generate maximum sales. But don't forget to allow for efficient aisles, corridors, and space for people to move in. Poor space planning just to maximize sales will lead to havoc on the floor during busy periods.

Turnover
Turnover refers to the number of times you fill every seat in the restaurant. For example, in a 150-seat restaurant, if you served 225 customers for lunch, then that would be a turnover rate of 1.5 for

that period. But use a daily total for the turnover number in this formula.

Average Guest Check

By referring to the preceding section of this chapter and by using Sample #5, the Restaurant Pyramid, you should have established a fairly accurate average of what each customer will spend. But you may have to consider some of the following points before coming to a final average: (a) What is the average amount that you yourself have spent in the same kind of restaurant? (b) Have you averaged in both lunch and dinner checks? (c) Will liquor increase the check? Try to establish a conservative amount here. No lender will believe an unusually high guest-check average; after all, they eat out too!

Operating Days

It's now time to plan how many days you'll be open. How about Sundays? Are you allowed to be open on Christmas or Easter? Are there lease restrictions? What can you see for the year ahead?

Using the formula, multiply the four items. This will give you your projected annual sales. And it is this number that will determine the economic viability of your new restaurant.

Cost of Sales

The serving of food and liquor is one of the most complicated forms of retailing because it includes manufacturing on the premises. Yes, manufacturing! And here's how it happens. Before a product reaches one of your customers, you must first buy the raw materials (fresh or frozen foods), process them, portion them, cook them, and then serve them to the customers, who must also be provided with a pleasant decor, furniture, glasses, plates, cutlery, and linen. You have already made a very heavy investment in equipment for refrigeration, cooking, and dishwashing. You have also employed cooks, dishwashers, bartenders, waiters, waitresses and hostesses, busboys, and janitors.

You deal in perishable goods; if you over-produce any item it may go to waste. You pay high prices for food because you have specified certain standards and delivery charges are added to the price.

Food Cost

Food sales on the statement (*see* Sample #7) refer to the total dollar volume, generated over a certain period of time (monthly, quarterly, yearly). These sales are based on the menu prices over the same period. Food cost is the total dollar volume of food that has been used over the same period. Food cost is generally stated through a percentage value determined by a formula.

$$\text{FORMULA} = \frac{\text{COST}}{\text{SALES}} \times 100\% = \text{Food Cost Percentage}$$

This percentage can be affected by many factors including: menu pricing, fluctuations in cost of food items, availability of product, portion control, waste, spoilage, and untrained staff.

Beverage Cost

Again, total beverage sales are the total volume over a certain reporting period. These sales figures are based on menu pricing over the same period. Beverage cost is the total dollar volume used to serve all of the beverages over the same period. Beverage cost is usually stated through a volume percentage determined by a formula.

$$\text{FORMULA} = \frac{\text{COST}}{\text{SALES}} \times 100\% = \text{Beverage Cost Percentage}$$

This percentage is influenced by many factors including: menu pricing, fluctuations in cost of beverage items, waste, spoilage, theft, portion control, and untrained staff. This beverage percentage is set at the outset through menu pricing. There are general average percentages for many kinds of restaurants, usually coordinated with menu food pricing to create a complimentary pricing structure. It is an important variable cost to increase your bottom line.

Labor Cost

Labor cost is also determined by the total dollar volume of payroll paid out to employees over a certain period, including all benefits. This value is applied against a total sales volume (through a formula) over the same period to arrive at a labor-cost percentage.

SAMPLE #6
Daily Labor Schedule—Licensed Deli Operation

	7 8 9 10 11 12 1 2 3 4 5 6 7 8 9 10 11 12 1 2	Hours	Rate	Total
Cooks —3 daily	X X X X X X X X X	8	14.00	112.00
	X X X X X X X X X	8	10.00	80.00
	X X X X X X X X X	8	6.50	52.00
Dishwasher —2 daily	X X X X X X X X X	8	5.00	40.00
	X X X X X X X X X	8	5.00	40.00
Take-out —6 daily	X X X X X X X X X	8	5.00	40.00
	X X X X X X X X X	8	5.00	40.00
	X X X X X X X X X	8	4.50	36.00
	X X X X X X X X X	8	4.50	36.00
	X X X X X X X X X	8	4.25	34.00
	X X X X X X X X X X	8	4.00	32.00
Counter —7 daily	X X X X X X X X X	8	7.50	60.00
	X X X X X X X X X	8	7.50	60.00
	X X X X X X X X X	8	7.00	56.00
	X X X X X X X X X	8	7.00	56.00
	X X X X X X X X X	8	6.50	52.00
	X X X X X X X X X	8	6.50	52.00
	X X X X X X X X X X	8	6.00	48.00
Servers —11 daily	X X X X X X X X X	8	4.50	36.00
	X X X X X X X X X	8	4.50	36.00
	X X X X X X X	6	4.50	27.00
	X X X X X X X	6	4.50	27.00
	X X X X X X X	6	4.50	27.00
	X X X X X X X	6	4.50	27.00
	X X X X X X X	6	4.50	27.00
	X X X X X X X	6	4.50	27.00
	X X X X X X X X X	8	4.50	36.00
	X X X X X X X X X	8	4.50	36.00
	X X X X X X X X X	8	4.50	36.00

SAMPLE #6 Continued

	11	12	1	2	3	4	5	6	7	8	9	10	11	12	1	2	Hours	Rate	Total
Bus-Boys —3 daily	X	X	X	X	X	X	X	X	X								8	4.50	36.00
	X	X	X	X	X	X	X	X	X								8	4.25	34.00
						X	X	X	X	X	X	X	X	X			8	4.00	32.00
Bartenders —2 daily	X	X	X	X	X	X	X	X	X								8	6.00	48.00
			X	X	X	X	X	X	X	X	X						8	6.00	48.00
Cashiers —2 daily	X	X	X	X	X	X	X	X	X								8	7.50	60.00
			X	X	X	X	X	X	X	X	X						8	7.50	60.00
Totals																	276		1,586.00

In other words, how much you paid out to all employees to generate so much sales expressed as a percentage value.

$$\text{FORMULA} = \frac{\text{Total Payroll}}{\text{Total Sales}} \times 100\% = \text{Labor Cost Percentage}$$

Labor costs vary greatly in the industry based on volume of food sold and setting price, menu variety, layout and design of restaurant, use of convenience foods, local wage rates, use of labor and equipment, hours of operation, and use of skilled or unskilled labor.

Again, the labor cost is a variable cost that is most important for the owner to control. Before opening, forecasting the work to be done through job descriptions and output expected from each new employee in every position is important. Also development of a staffing guideline through scheduling by category is an important tool. Sample #6 shows you how to determine what your labor cost will be in a new operation.

The Hidden Costs

Now that we have determined how to establish your sales and have worked out your food and labor costs, there is one area left to analyze: hidden costs.

We call these costs hidden because, unlike the food and labor costs, which are very visible to both you and your customer, these costs are not only unseen, but are very often forgotten by the new restaurateur. They can make the difference between success and failure.

Most of these costs are normally fixed and bear no relation to your sales volume. For example, if you are paying $1,000 per month in rent and have sales of $10,000, your percentage is 10 percent. If your sales drop to $5,000 per month, your rent is still $1,000, but now represents 20 percent of your sales. Therefore, you have to know what these hidden costs are before you can determine if your operation is going to be successful.

Let us analyze each of these hidden costs and see how they might relate to you.

Rent

1. Is the rent fixed, is it calculated as a percentage of sales, or is it both with a minimum base?
2. Is the rent based on actual square footage or is it pro-rated to include a portion of the common area?
3. Do you have to pay C.A.M.?
4. Do you have to pay F.A.M.?
5. Do you have to pay Merchants Association dues?
6. Are there any other extras?

Realty/Property Taxes

1. Are these included in the rent or are they an additional cost?
2. Do you pay directly or does the landlord pay and bill you back at cost or up-charge?
3. Do you have to pay a portion of the common-area taxes as well?
4. Downtown taxes can be very high. Never take the landlord's word; find out what they are yourself.

Business Taxes
These are assessed against your business. Call the local authorities and find out what a similar business in your area pays.

Advertising
Normally a percentage of sales (approximately 5 percent) is allowed for advertising. If business is good you may not wish to spend that

much; then again, if business is poor you may have to spend more. It is very important to set up a budget allowing for slow and busy times so that in the end you reach your budget figure.

Legal and Accounting
The legal fees may only come once a year, but you must allow for them. Accounting is broken down into two areas:

1. Annual return by your accountant.
2. Ongoing bookkeeping, including general ledger and payroll.

Insurance
Again, a once-a-year item, but make sure you allow for it. Check your lease requirements.

Telephone
A monthly item, but remember a business phone costs more than a residential one.

Credit Card Charges
If you accept credit cards you will be charged 4 percent to 5 percent on all receipts, so you have to estimate how much of your business will be by this payment method. Note that the higher the average guest check, the more charge cards are used.

Utilities
1. Electricity: What kind of cooking equipment will you be using?
2. Gas: What kind of heating will you have?
   (a) If in a mall, does the landlord pay or do you?
   (b) Do you have a meter or is it estimated?
   (c) Would you be better off to get your own meter?
   (d) If you are running a deli, you would not use much in the way of gas or electricity.
3. Water and Sewage: Is this included or are you billed separately?

Replacement Costs
Replacement costs can be a very high item in a sit-down family restaurant (up to 1 percent), but very low in a fast-food outlet.

Repairs and Maintenance

In a new restaurant this cost will be low during the first year, since your equipment will be under warranty. In an existing restaurant it could be much higher, depending on the age and condition of the equipment. Never save money in this area at the expense of the customer.

Laundry, Linen, and Uniforms

1. Can be a very high expense if you use linen tablecloths and napkins.
2. Allow for uniform rental and laundry for kitchen staff.
3. Will serving staff wear uniforms? If so, how will they be cleaned? Staff never do a good job themselves unless you are very strict. Different laundering methods can result in different shades of color in the uniforms.

General Contracts

1. Cleaning the Restaurant: Who? How much? How often? Do you have the necessary equipment?
2. Window Cleaning: Can this be done yourself? Will you remember? Do you have the equipment?
3. Snow Removal: What kind of contract, per time or per season? What about sidewalks?
4. Pest Control: Don't wait until there is a problem; the cheapest isn't always the best. Will your contractor make recommendations?
5. Carpet Cleaning or Rental: May be a necessity in the winter.
6. Exhaust Canopies: Annual cleaning for safety and efficiency.
7. Drains: Will there be a lot of grease? (You bet.) Some malls may insist on providing a regular maintenance program and charge you back.
8. Waste Removal: Mall or city may insist on a bin. How often will you need it emptied? Will there be an odor problem? Where will bin be placed?

Office Expenses

Allow for guest checks, cash register tapes, bookkeeping supplies, stationary, postage, control forms, inventory sheets, and other materials.

Paper Supplies

1. To include the cost of menus, placemats, napkins, table tents, bar supplies, and coasters.
2. If you have a fast-food take-out then your costs will include paper plates, cups, take-out boxes, bags, plastic cutlery, and sauce containers.

Bank Charges and Interest

Cost of maintaining a business account, interest on loans or lines of credit.

In summary, the total of all hidden costs should not come to more than 20 percent of your entire cost. If it does, can you realistically see any profit from your operation?

Now that we have evaluated food, labor, and other costs, we should be showing a return on our operation before debt service, that is, paying back the loan. This is what your bank manager or money lender wants to see. Your ability to borrow money will depend on what you have projected in this area, and how realistic that projection is.

This bottom line will also be very important if you ever want to sell your business. It will tell the buyer what kind of return can be expected on an investment and, therefore, will help to determine how much he or she will offer for the business. It also tells you what your investment is worth and how well you can expect to run your operation.

The Breakeven Projection

When drawing up a plan for a new business, it is always a good practice to consider the downside. In preparing a breakeven projection, you are really trying to ascertain how low the sales can be before you go out of business. By preparing this projection, you are also showing the lender that you have anticipated the worst and that you will know when your business is in trouble. In putting together this statement, there are certain principles that you will have to remember. Although your food cost should remain at a constant percentage, your labor percentage will grow higher. This happens because your operation cannot run properly without a minimum staff complement. Also, many of your hidden costs are fixed, such as base rent or insurance, so these figures will remain the same (*see* Sample #7).

Three-to-Five-Year Projections

This sheet (*see* Sample #8) is basically an extension of the first year's projection. Whether this projection should be over three, five, or more years depends on the amount of money you are borrowing and the length of the repayment period.

The two main principles to remember are that sales should show a steady increase and that you will have to allow for a higher dollar cost on labor, food, and other expenses. Sales will increase because of general price increases on your menu and because your customer count will grow as your business becomes established. Although expenses will also rise, if you are operating your business properly, your bottom line will show a slight percentage increase to cover you against inflation.

Cash Flow Pro-Forma

The need for a cash flow pro-forma is more for your own benefit, although your lender or investor may want this projection prepared as well. It establishes when cash will actually be required, especially during the construction or renovation stage and in the first months of operation when there may be a need for cash to cover an initial operation loss. Sample #9 shows progress payments during construction as well as salaries paid out during the pre-opening training period. It also assumes that all your initial orders from suppliers are C.O.D., a normal practice for a new operator, but that after the initial orders, your suppliers are allowing you to pay on receipt of statement or net 15 days.

Statement of Net Worth

The personal statement of net worth is simply a total of your assets minus the total of your liabilities (*see* Sample #10). If you are going into partnership with others, your lender may require net worth statements for them as well. Again, this will depend on the amount of money you are borrowing and what type of partnership arrangement you have or will have structured. Regardless of the total of your declared net worth, your lender will discount the net amount by 25 percent to 50 percent. This is done because, in the event of bankruptcy, your assets would not realize their worth as stated if they had to be sold off quickly.

SAMPLE #7
Breakeven Projected Operating Statement (Mall Location)

	Jan.	Feb.	Mar.	April	May	June	July	Aug.	Sept.	Oct.	Nov.	Dec.	Total	%
Sales	13,000	11,400	13,000	14,250	14,250	13,700	12,500	12,500	14,250	14,800	17,100	19,250	170,000	100.0
Cost of Sales	4,550	3,990	4,550	4,990	4,990	4,795	4,375	4,375	4,985	5,180	5,985	6,735	59,500	35.0
Labor	4,000	3,800	4,000	4,000	4,000	4,000	4,000	4,000	4,000	4,200	5,000	5,000	50,000	29.4
Total Cost of Sales	8,550	7,790	8,550	8,990	8,990	8,795	8,375	8,375	8,985	9,380	10,985	11,735	109,500	64.4
Gross Margin	4,450	3,610	4,450	5,260	5,260	4,905	4,125	4,125	5,265	5,420	6,115	7,515	60,500	35.6
OTHER EXPENSES:														
Base Rent	1,700	1,700	1,700	1,700	1,700	1,700	1,700	1,700	1,700	1,700	1,700	1,700	20,400	12.0
Percentage Rent	—	—	—	—	—	—	—	—	—	—	—	—	—	—
C.A.M./F.A.M.	520	520	520	520	520	520	520	520	520	520	520	520	6,240	3.6
Realty Taxes	310	310	310	310	310	310	310	310	310	310	310	310	3,720	2.2
Business Taxes	—	—	—	500	—	500	—	500	—	500	—	—	2,000	1.2
Advertising	625	625	625	625	625	625	625	625	625	625	625	625	7,500	4.4
Legal & Accounting	—	—	—	—	—	—	—	—	—	—	—	3,000	3,000	1.8
Insurance	700	—	—	—	—	—	—	—	—	—	—	—	700	0.4
Telephone	35	35	35	35	35	35	35	35	35	35	35	35	420	0.2
Utilities	330	330	330	330	330	330	330	330	330	330	330	330	3,960	2.3
Replacement Costs	—	—	75	—	—	75	—	—	75	—	—	75	300	0.2
Repairs & Maintenance	100	100	100	100	100	100	100	100	100	100	100	100	1,200	0.7
Cleaning Supplies	25	25	25	25	25	25	25	25	25	25	25	25	300	0.2
Laundry, Linen & Uniforms	40	40	40	40	40	40	40	40	40	40	40	40	480	0.3

													Total	%
Pest Control	15	15	15	15	15	15	15	15	15	15	15	15	180	0.1
Drain Cleaning	10	10	10	10	10	10	10	10	10	10	10	10	120	0.1
General Office & Bookkeeping	100	100	100	100	100	100	100	100	100	100	100	100	1,200	0.7
Bank Charges	25	15	15	15	15	15	15	15	15	15	20	20	200	0.1
Paper Supplies	650	570	650	710	710	685	625	625	715	740	855	965	8,500	5.0
Total Other Expenses	5,185	4,395	4,550	5,035	4,535	5,085	4,450	4,950	4,615	5,065	4,685	7,870	60,420	35.5
Net Profit (Loss)	(735)	(785)	(100)	225	725	(180)	(325)	(825)	650	355	1,430	(355)	80	.1
Loan Repayment (P&I)	?	?	?	?	?	?	?	?	?	?	?	?	?	?
Cash Surplus (Deficit)	?	?	?	?	?	?	?	?	?	?	?	?	?	?

SAMPLE #8
3 Year Projected Statement of Operation
(Mall Location)

	Year One	Year Two	Year Three
Sales	300,000	350,000	390,000
Cost of Sales	105,000 (35%)	122,500 (35%)	136,500 (35%)
Labor Cost	75,000 (25%)	82,500 (23.6%)	90,500 (23.2%)
Total Cost of Sales	180,000 (60%)	205,000 (58.6%)	227,000 (58.2%)
Gross Margin	120,000 (40%)	145,000 (41.4%)	163,000 (41.8%)
OTHER EXPENSES			
Base Rent	20,400	20,400	20,400
Percentage Rent	3,600	7,600	10,800
C.A.M./F.A.M.	6,240	6,900	7,500
Realty Taxes	3,720	4,100	4,500
Business Taxes	2,000	2,200	2,400
Advertising	7,500	8,750	10,000
Legal & Accounting	3,000	3,300	3,600
Insurance	700	800	900
Telephone	420	480	540
Utilities	3,960	4,320	4,800
Replacement Costs	300	330	360
Repairs & Maintenance	1,200	1,320	1,450
Cleaning Supplies	300	330	360
Laundry, Linen & Uniforms	750	840	930
Pest Control	180	200	220
Drain Cleaning	120	—	—
Office Expenses/ Bookkeeping	1,200	1,320	1,450
Bank Charges	200	220	240
Paper Supplies & Printing	15,000	17,500	19,500
Total Expenses	70,790 (23.6%)	81,050 (23.2%)	90,110 (23.1%)
Net Profit (Loss)	49,210 (16.4%)	63,950 (18.2%)	72,890 (18.7%)
Loan Repayment (P.&I.)	?	?	?
Cash Surplus (Deficit)	?	?	?

SAMPLE #9

Any Restaurant

Cash Flow-Projection

Target Opening—May 1st 1986

	Jan.	Feb.	Mar.	April	May	June	July	Aug.
In-Flows								
Sales	—	—	—	—	15,000	18,000	19,000	22,000
Bank Loan	—	—	—	60,000	—	—	—	—
Personal Investment	70,000	—	—	—	—	—	—	—
Surplus Cash B/F*	—	65,000	44,000	19,000	29,000	11,250	9,310	7,980
TOTAL	70,000	65,000	44,000	79,000	44,000	29,250	28,310	29,980
Out-Flows								
Development Costs	5,000	—	—	—	—	—	—	—
Construction & Improvements	—	20,000	14,000	17,000	9,000	—	—	—
Equipment & Furnishing	—	—	10,000	15,000	5,000	—	—	—
Cost of Sales	—	—	—	5,000	6,000	7,200	7,600	8,800
Labor Costs	—	—	—	2,000	6,000	6,000	6,000	6,000
Other Costs	—	1,000	1,000	11,000	5,000	5,000	5,000	5,000
Loan Interest	—	—	—	—	750	740	730	720
Loan Reduction	—	—	—	—	1,000	1,000	1,000	1,000
TOTAL	5,000	21,000	25,000	50,000	32,750	19,940	20,330	21,520
Cash Surplus C/F*	65,000	44,000	19,000	29,000	11,250	9,310	7,980	8,460

* B/F—Brought Forward
* C/F—Carried Forward

SAMPLE #10

Statement of Net Worth

ASSETS

Primary Residence

Market Value	$100,000.00	
Less 1st Mortgage	50,000.00	
		$50,000.00
Automobile		6,000.00
Household Contents		20,000.00
Jewelry & Paintings (Appraised Value)		15,000.00
Stocks & Bonds		8,000.00
Term Deposits (Name of Bank)		10,000.00
Savings Account		2,000.00
Current Account		1,500.00
Total Assets:		$112,500.00

LIABILITIES

Charge Card Balance (Visa)	1,200.00
Bank Loan (Name of Bank)	2,000.00
Total Liabilities	3,200.00
TOTAL NET WORTH	$109,300.00

Company Structure

Regardless of whether you are going into business by yourself, taking in one or more partners, or having twenty outsiders invest in your business, you should detail the company structure and the role, if any, that each person will play in the running of the company. If, for example, one of your investors is an accountant and it has been decided that this person will act as company treasurer, then put this information under this section. It will undoubtedly add weight to your proposal. In fact, the accountant will probably prepare your business plan and accompany you when you apply for that loan.

Personal Résumés

The résumé is a brief history of your business and, if applicable, educational background. Emphasis should be placed on any food-industry or business background that would show expertise in the field into which you are planning to enter. Résumés should also be included for any other partners or principals who are entering the business with you.

Presentation of the Proposal

The presentation of the proposal should not be ignored. Follow the principles used by the leading manufacturers of consumer goods and remember that good packaging helps to sell the product. The proposal should be professionally typed and xerox bound. This can be done at a very small cost by any of the many quick-print companies now in operation. Artistic renderings or photographs of the proposed operation will add to your packaging. The more professional the proposal, the more impressed your lender will be with you.

Summary

The following is a summary of what your business plan should include:

1. An Outline of Your Business:
   — Why this particular type of restaurant?
   — Where is it located and why?
   — Who is the landlord? Include copy of lease.
   — When do you plan to open? Include timetable.
   — How will you make it succeed?
2. Start-Up Costs:
   — Construction/renovation/buying price
   — Fixtures/furnishings/equipment
   — Legal/accounting/development
   — Inventory/pre-opening costs
   — Cash to cover delays and slow openings
   — Allowance for cost of over-runs
3. First Twelve Months Operating Projections:
   — Sales—seasonal highs and lows
   — Food Cost—constant percentage
   — Labor Cost—allow for vacation pay, minimum rate increases, employer contributions
   — Other Costs—percentage rent constant with sales
   — Loan repayment
   — Separate sheets on how you arrived at these figures

4. Breakeven Projection:
   — An operating projection for the first 12 months showing how low your sales can drop before you start losing money.
5. Three-to-Five-Year Projection:
   — Extension of No. 3
   — Show steady growth
   — Allow for price increases
6. Cash Flow Pro-Forma:
   — Shows actual flow of cash
   — Allow for payables
   — Show all monies in and out and when
7. Statement of Personal Net Worth:
   — Assets less liabilities = Net Worth
   — Shows your personal ability to repay the loan
8. Company Structure:
   — If more than one person in company
   — Nature of setup or arrangement
9. Personal Résumés:
   — Your background
   — Background of other company members
10. Presentation:
   — Good packaging to sell
   — Shows a professional approach

5

SHOPPING FOR MONEY

Defining the Need

If you have enough money to open your own business, then you've already overcome your biggest hurdle. Yet, you will still have to analyze it to see if it makes good business sense.

Let us consider that you have $100,000, and that that amount is exactly what you require to fulfill your dream. At the present interest rates your money, in a very safe term deposit, will earn approximately $9,000 each year. Add to this your present income of $24,933 from your regular employment (the present American average), and the total is $33,933. Your restaurant should return you more than the total of this sum because of the risk factor. By staying as you are, you not only have an income of $33,933, but your $100,000 is perfectly safe. By investing in a restaurant, you may lose your money and be unemployed, so there should be a compensating factor.

Alas, people rarely use good business sense when trying to fulfill a dream. Your shopping list, or business plan, defines exactly what your financial requirements are, and how you will use the money. Now you are ready to go shopping, but where do you start?

The Sources

Family and Friends
Loans from family and friends are probably the cheapest form of borrowing, with the least pressure to repay if things aren't going too

well. However, you should still approach this form of borrowing in a professional manner. Your business plan will show that you have completed your homework and will inspire a lot more confidence in the friends or relatives you approach for help. After all, no matter how well the lender knows you, they still want to make sure that they will be repaid.

You must also consider the situation where your business is unsuccessful. Even if you are not legally required to repay the loan, there may be a very strong moral obligation to do so, or you risk losing a friend. You may also be surprised at the interest the friend or relative shows in your business, especially if you are struggling.

Active Partners

A partnership is like a marriage; you have to be sure from the beginning that you can work together and that each can take and give constructive criticism. The working arrangement also has to be worked out in advance. The partnership agreement should be in writing, in order to facilitate an amicable way to dissolve it, should it prove unworkable (*see* Chapter 10).

Case Study—Partners

On his birthday, Ted was out celebrating the fact that in just two short weeks, his restaurant would be opening. Well, not *his* exactly. He'd been working on the concept alone for almost a year, and had come up short every time he figured out his budget.

At first he'd been discouraged. It looked as though his idea was dead, when he suddenly thought of taking a partner, or maybe even two. That way he'd still have his own restaurant, run it his way, and risk even less capital than he'd planned.

He began by approaching his friends and relatives, but either they couldn't see him as a restaurateur, or didn't believe in the concept. So he began to look outside of his own circle for a partner. And he found one.

His first partner, an insurance salesman, was a bit older than Ted. He was willing to put up the same money as Ted, dollar for dollar, but he wanted to be actively involved in the management of the restaurant. This was okay with Ted because he realized that everyone wanted to watch his investment.

Then the two of them went looking for more capital. One of the new partner's former insurance clients was a rich businessman, and after a few meetings, he, too, chose to come in as a silent partner. Just as an investment, he said, and so he would have a place to come for business entertaining.

So far so good, Ted thought. I've given up two-thirds of the company and control, but at least I'm opening up. The second company could be all mine, he reasoned. After the first one is open and running properly . . .

One year later, on his birthday, Ted was out of work, and wondering just where he'd gone wrong. There had been clues before he'd opened, but what were they? He just couldn't say.

The active partner had gone bad on him right at the start, fiddling with the staff and partying all the time. Ted had learned that trying to teach the business, give direction, and apply some discipline were impossible when dealing with a partner. At the weekly owner's meetings, the businessman always sided with the insurance man. Ted was out-voted every time on menu and price changes. Even the quality of the food was changed against his advice. His partners wanted profits at any cost, and had no interest in market longevity. The businessman's son was working behind the bar now, not the place for a spoiled brat to be—dealing with the public.

It hadn't been right, and Ted's continued voicing of the wrongs went unheeded at meetings.

Eventually, the partners had simply fired him. Oh, he still owned a third of the company, but he had no control over his investment. The other two were running it now.

As Ted hoisted another beer, he realized that although it had cost less money to open his restaurant by using partners, it had been too expensive in the long run. He'd lost charge and now someone else had control of his dream.

Silent Partners

The one thing you can be sure of with silent partners is that they are never silent! In a majority of cases, they are not familiar with the business, and their questions may become very frustrating because they often lack understanding.

They can hold their position in your company by way of preferred share which would have to be redeemed. In other words, their investment is repayable, plus they may also retain part ownership by way of common shares (*see* Chapter 10).

Silent partners usually like to be kept informed. To avoid constant phone calls and visits from partners, it is always advisable to set up a regular monthly meeting, where you can report the progress or lack of it during the previous month. If approached in the correct manner, these meetings can be very productive, and depending on the business background of your partners, you could receive valuable help and suggestions drawn from their prior experience.

Banks

If you are approaching your local bank manager, you must realize that his or her personal limit on granting loans may only be ten or twenty thousand dollars. As you will probably need more than this amount, your application for financing may require a regional or head office approval. The person dealing with your application will, therefore, probably have no personal knowledge of you or your past business background. This factor should emphasize the importance of your business plan, as this is what your application will be judged upon.

Regardless of how profitable your business proposal looks, the bank will always look on the downside, or how you will repay the loan if things go wrong. Consequently, they will require some, or all of the following as security:

1. the assets of your business
2. your personal guarantee
3. your personal assets, i.e., house, car, etc.
4. third-party guarantee

To ascertain whether your personal guarantee is of value, your statement of net worth (*see* Chapter 4), will be analyzed and probably discounted by 25 percent to 50 percent. This discount factor is used because the banks have to consider the amount they would realize from your assets if they had to be sold off quickly in a bankruptcy situation.

City/State—Small Business Loans

City and state "small business loans" have varying criteria, depending on where you live. But regardless of this factor, the underlying purpose of these loans is job creation. Consequently, your business proposal should emphasize this fact—how many new jobs will be created, what training you are able to give in developing new skills or, by increasing the capacity of your existing business, how may additional jobs will be created.

Credit Unions

Credit unions usually provide mortgages, but many are now moving into other areas of financing. However, the normal prerequisite is that you be a member. If you are, it may be worth a meeting with your local manager; if not, you may wish to investigate the advantages, if any, of joining.

Leasing

This area of financing has grown rapidly over the last few years. Many of the major banks are involved, either directly or through subsidiaries.

The leasing company either owns, services, insures, repairs and maintains the equipment, or just owns it and you take care of the rest. Many equipment companies will tell you the kind of companies involved with leasing, but although this type of financing can greatly reduce your start-up costs, it will increase your ongoing monthly fixed costs, unless you structure some sort of buy-out agreement. Even so, you will find that it will cost you more in the long run.

Suppliers

Financing from suppliers is not as common now as it once was. As an example of this type of financing, there was a time when major fish-suppliers would help set up take-out fish-and-chip stores by way of equipment and loans. This help was given on the condition that the operator would purchase the product from the supplier. In this way, the supplier would create a market for its product. This form of business has now evolved into franchising. It is unlikely that you will be able to obtain capital in this manner today, unless the product you are planning to sell is very unique.

Franchisors

Many franchise companies can either provide financing themselves, or through a bank or finance company that is already familiar with their operation. Regardless of the arrangements they may have in place, you will have to show your ability to repay, if things go wrong.

Venture Capital Companies

Venture capital companies do not normally get involved with new businesses. They will often get involved when a company gets into trouble, because they feel that with the right amount of cash and management expertise they can turn things around. For this input, they will normally require an equity position. This type of financing is not usually available for single-restaurant operations.

Going Public

Again, this is not for the first-time, single operation. It takes time and money, so wait until you have a chain of restaurants, then talk to your lawyer.

Tips on Dealing with Banks

Banks will always look at your past record when you are applying for a loan. If this is your first business venture they can only view your personal transactions. In either instance try to follow some of these tips:

1. Always try to borrow when you don't need it, so as to establish a good record of repayment.
2. If you have a line of credit, never leave it stagnant; work it down then let it go up again. Lack of activity makes a manager uncomfortable.
3. Invite your bank manager to your premises occasionally. It will give him or her a greater understanding of your business which will help in future dealings.
4. If things get tough, let your manager know early. Never leave it to the last minute. Your manager may be able to give good advice. Remember, he or she has your best interests at heart.
5. Keep your bank manager informed on a regular basis, especially if things are going well, and try to put things in writing, i.e., copies of monthly statements, etc. You will gain your bank manager's respect and trust, and he or she will be more inclined to help if things get tough or you wish to expand.

In conclusion, remember that when you are shopping for money, nobody is going to lend you more than you are willing to risk yourself, unless they can have control, and then the advantages of going into business for yourself are gone.

6

LOCATION, LOCATION, LOCATION

The Exception and the Rule

An entrepreneur once said, "The three most important factors in a restaurant's success are location, location, location."

1. *The Exception*—The selection of the location might not be quite as important as it once was. We all know of a restaurant that seems to be in a very poor location and yet is very successful. But this restaurant is successful *in spite of* its location, not *because* of it. It has probably spent a considerable amount of time and money advertising its location and building up its customers, as well as providing good food and service to keep them.
2. *The Rule*—But these restaurants are the exception, not the rule. The major foodservice chains spend millions of dollars each year to find the right locations, and many of the smaller companies just follow the example of the big guys. When McDonald's opens a new location, others will follow its lead. They reason that McDonald's must have done its homework.

What You Can Do

So, what can you do to ensure you pick the right location? You obviously don't have the same resources as the large food chains, and opening up next to a McDonald's or a Burger King may not be the right solution either. Well, you can follow the same procedures as the large companies, and although it may take you longer, the time taken now can be the difference between success and failure in the future.

Be Objective

When looking for a location, you must be objective and impassionate. Judging with only their heart and eyes only is the way most people buy houses and cars, and is probably the reason that so many poor decisions are made in these areas. You have to look for the potential in a restaurant location, and what it will be like when you have finished with it, not what it's like at the moment. You have to listen to what people say, and then decide or investigate for yourself. And most important of all, you must not rush or get frustrated if you don't immediately find what you know you want.

Case Study #1—Location

Sam and Janet Smith often talked about owning their own restaurant, especially when they were out for dinner. Most of the restaurants in their area were busy during dinner hour, they noticed. The customers were of all types—singles, couples, and families.

"If we could find the right place, we could open our own restaurant and make a good dollar in this business," Janet said.

"That's right," Sam agreed. "A family-style restaurant, specializing in Italian food. I'd look after the out-front part. Hell, we'd just need a small place really. Home-cooked meals, and at low prices too."

And so they began to look for a location, but after two months of looking, they were frustrated. There was just nothing right for them in their immediate area.

A real estate agent who knew they were looking called them one day with an excited pitch. "It's a beauty, Sam. It's over on Elm Street, you know, near that industrial park about eight miles away. It's in a strip plaza, and there's tons of space available, too. The rents are surprisingly reasonable as well."

Sam and Janet went to see the location, and sure enough, there were only two stores rented in the plaza. They could have their pick of any of the other eight spots, and the parking lot was large and with good access.

Beside the plaza was a large manufacturing company and many other businesses and companies in the industrial park that Elm Street bisected.

"It's a great location," said the real estate agent. "Just look at the hundreds of people working around here. You'll be jammed all the time. And think of all the people coming into the area on business. There's plenty of parking for them all."

Sam and Janet agreed, and they rented the location.

Two months later, after raising money from savings and taking out a second mortgage on their house, they were open.

Opening day, all of Sam's and Janet's friends came to the new restaurant which they called S&J's. It was a sit-down, 85-seat, full-menu-style operation, open from 10:00 A.M. to 10:00 P.M. each day.

The problems began on the second day.

With only 85 seats, they filled up every day for lunch. Janet's specials and regular menu items were well prepared and served, and the response was very good at first. But for the customers who came after the restaurant was full, there was a long wait. Janet's meals were always made from scratch and cooked to order—no frozen or convenience foods for S&J's. So the restaurant just couldn't turn people over fast enough. There just wasn't enough time. The hundreds of people in the area were on fixed lunch hours. They didn't have time to wait for service so lunch business fell off.

And the expected dinner trade?

Well, everyone in the immediate area left for home by 5:00 P.M. The restaurant's location was in the middle of an industrial park and there was no residential area to draw from. The area was deserted by 6:00 P.M. each day, and it was empty on the weekends.

Sam and Janet were disappointed and in financial trouble. "Maybe we can change our hours," Janet said. "You know, open at 7:00 A.M. for breakfasts and coffee breaks, and add a take-out service."

"Yes," said Sam, "We should have realized that this area isn't a dinner-trade area. This mall has been open almost a year now and the only other tenants so far are a quick printing house and a dry cleaner. I guess their marketing approach was better than ours in finding a location. Maybe we should have looked longer, or known what style of restaurant would have worked better in this location."

Case Study #1—Critique

When we review the mistakes Sam and Janet made, we see that although each one was small in itself, added together they greatly contributed to the demise of the business.

1. They became frustrated after only two months when they could not find a location in their area. But looking for the right location is cheap. The only expense was their spare time and gas. There was no rush!

2. The real estate agent became excited at the location he had found, and that contagious enthusiasm was passed on to Sam and Janet. They forgot that this man was a salesman and that his job is to sell. Creating enthusiasm is part of his selling technique.

3. The location they selected was eight miles away from where they lived. They did not know the area, or take any time to study the traffic patterns throughout each day or week.

4. There were only two other stores rented in the plaza, which had been available to rent for over a year. Sam and Janet should have asked themselves why no one else had rented the available stores, and why these two particular stores were successful.

5. The area was an industrial park, with high-traffic density during business hours—the reason for the success of the two service stores. Sam and Janet were relying not only on a lunch trade, but also on evening business. But they failed to realize that the area was deserted during the evenings and on weekends because there was no residential traffic.

6. Their menu format of cooking fresh items to order was admirable, but the lunchtime patrons were on a tight schedule and could not afford the time to wait.

7. Finally, Sam and Janet had to adapt their restaurant operation, at further expense, to the area. It would have been less costly if they had found the right location in the first place.

Traffic Flow

In scouting your proposed location, you must consider traffic flow and its patterns around your site. You'll have to be on-site looking and studying access to and from the site in both directions and around you on side streets. Begin each morning and make notes following the checklist below:

1. Which streets around you have the heavy commuter flow?
2. In which directions, and at what peak times daily?
3. When cars turn off the street, do they cause a bottleneck?
4. Are cars reluctant to turn against a major flow?

5. What about the cars turning onto your street?
6. How about bus and streetcar traffic?
7. Do they have trouble with traffic? And at what times?
8. Are there large employee parking lots that empty onto the street at shift-change times?
9. Are there medians that will cut off traffic onto your site?
10. Are there turn lanes?
11. Or no turn signs that will keep customers away?
12. How about stoplights?
13. Are there yield signs that make it difficult to cross?
14. Is your street one-way, and will it prevent traffic flow?
15. Are there major traffic highways going by?
16. Are you blocked by access ramps to these highways?
17. What is the future of traffic in the area?
18. What do merchants have to say about traffic in the area?

Parking

This item is often underestimated by new restaurateurs. Yet it is very important to remember that customers want the most convenient method of getting close to their choice of restaurant, especially during bad weather. Scout the new location thoroughly and watch for peak demand upon your own lot, if you have one.

1. Is there off-street parking for your customers?
2. Or are you going to provide it at a paid lot?
3. Do you have to share a lot with other businesses?
4. Are you required to provide parking by your municipality?
5. Who'll pay for maintenance cost on that lot?
6. Is it a city-run lot? With parking meters?
7. Or a private lot? Will you validate for your customers?
8. Who'll plow your lot in winter? Who'll paint, line, and resurface it?
9. Is there street parking out front? At what costs? And times?
10. Where will your delivery trucks park?
11. Is there an alley behind you for receiving?
12. Are garbage trucks going to be able to get into your bins?
13. Is there heated underground parking?
14. If you share the lot, what are the peak times for other businesses?
15. Are there already problems in your lot with space?

16. Can you really do without parking for your customers?
17. How far away is the lot from your front door?
18. Who'll shovel a pathway to your front door?
19. What is the future of parking in the area?
20. What do merchants in the area have to say about parking?

Residential

Within your proposed concept package, you'll have discovered what kind of customer profile you'll need to support your new restaurant. So, do they live around you? You'll have to walk around the neighborhood completely, making notes on the things you see. Be sure to look on weekends as well as weekdays. Everyone's home sometime.

1. What kind of residences are around you?
2. Single-family houses? Townhouses? High-rise buildings? Duplexes? Condos?
3. Are there rental units around you? At what price ranges?
4. Are they geared to families? Seniors? Singles?
5. What are their occupancy rates?
6. How long have they been open and renting?
7. How much of a walk is it to your site?
8. Do they have tenant parking?
9. Will they have to drive to your location?
10. Can you estimate the disposable income of these residents?
11. Are there new developments going into the area?
12. What kind? When are they due to open?
13. Is the area increasing in density?

Commercial

It is important to look at the commercial makeup of the area, especially when considering growth. Businesses around your restaurant will be generators of customers, as well.

1. What kinds of businesses are there in your area?
2. How are they doing?
3. How long have they been there?
4. What businesses have folded around you? Why?
5. What kind of customer profile were they based on?
6. Is their customer profile the same as yours?
7. Are your customer counts the same as theirs?

8. What new businesses have just moved in? Why?
9. What businesses depend upon traffic flow to survive?
10. Are there other service businesses in your area?
11. Are they on the increase?
12. Is their marketing the same as yours?
13. Can you piggyback onto their marketing strategy and locate there?
14. What other businesses in your own building are there?
15. Are they successful?
16. How are sales around you?
17. Are they on the decline? or increase?
18. Does everyone go home after 5:00 P.M.? What will that do to your dinner hour?
19. How many store windows have a sale on? Why?
20. Are there commercial developments coming in?
21. How will they affect your customer counts if they have restaurants?
22. What businesses have just moved into this development?
23. Does the area generate pedestrian traffic?
24. Is there a local merchants organization? With statistics on the area?
25. Are there farmers' markets? What days will they generate traffic?
26. Does the area have a theme-style sales period? Octoberfest-style? Is the area on the increase?

Competition

This scouting of your prospective competitors is not underhanded or sneaky at all. You must know how the customers in the area buy, at what times, and so forth. This information is important to measure against your own customer profile and concept. It is wise, however, to be very modest in your approach.

1. What is your competition in the area?
2. How many kinds of restaurants are there and in what locations around you?
3. What is their marketing strategy?
4. How long have they been there?
5. What others have gone broke in the area? Why?
6. Who is coming into the area? Why?
7. How are your competitors' sales?

8. Their customer counts?
9. Menu-style and pricing?
10. Average guest check?
11. Customer profile?
12. Turnover?
13. When are their rush periods?
14. How is their service and quality?
15. Goodwill within the neighborhood?
16. Management styles?
17. Customer parking?
18. Have you forecasted their sales?
19. Hours of operation?
20. Take-out business?
21. Walk-in trade?
22. Are they expanding? Why?
23. Are they independent? Or a chain?
24. What sort of controls do you see in place? How are their employees?
25. What do others say about the competition? Are there complaints? Why?
26. Is the area saturated with restaurants? Same type as yours? Why? Or are there just too many in general?
27. Can you take over some of their business?
28. How much advertising do your competitors do? Why? Where?
29. Is it an ongoing program? Why?
30. Do they offer specials? Discounts? Coupons? Why?
31. Are their hours the same as yours will be?
32. Are they trendy places?
33. Is their volume built on liquor sales? Why?
34. Are you the same?
35. Are you trying to copy someone in the area? Why?
36. Can you do better? Do you have the budget to improve on them?
37. Will any competitors discuss their operations with you?
38. Are they restricted by local by-laws? Will you be also?
39. Are the area's restaurants on the decline? Or increase?
40. What is the feel of the competition?
41. Do they match the area? Or are their customers coming from outside?
42. Will yours?

43. Will you compliment your new neighborhood?
44. Will your menu pricing fit your new area?
45. Will your food items fit also?

Municipal Regulations

Many local regulations and by-laws can govern your proposed new venture. You should be aware of all of them. Find out at City Hall just which ones apply to you.

1. Is your location within the municipality restricted in any way?
2. Are there parking requirements?
3. Occupancy requirements? Building restrictions? Restaurant licenses?
4. State liquor board restrictions?
5. Landlord restrictions?
6. Is the municipality planning any developments in your area?
7. Are highways coming in?
8. Cut-offs for that highway? Or by-passes?
9. Is new housing coming in? Commerical developments? Growth? Decline?
10. Will changing by-laws affect traffic, parking, commercial areas?
11. Are sewers coming? Road resurfacing? And taxes to pay for them?
12. Is urban renewal coming? Expropriation?
13. Will there be new recreation centers? Sports complexes? Farmers' markets?
14. Parade routings? Theme sales periods?
15. Are there churches or schools in the area? Are you too close to them for a liquor license?
16. Have other restaurants been successfully opposed when they applied for a liquor license?
17. Will you be able to alleviate the worries of concerned citizens?
18. Are there municipal or area demographic reports?
19. Or surveys of growth or decline?
20. How is the zoning?
21. Can you afford the time and money to fight a zoning change through City Hall.
22. Does the area feel right for your proposed operation?
23. What does the future hold for your community as a whole?

24. Is your community successfully fighting off the recessions that come along? Or is it suffering?

Research Others Can Do

Once you have completed all the areas of research that you can do, it is worth considering other sources of help that you may be able to enlist.

Bank Manager
Your bank manager, or the local branch manager, if you are planning to locate out of your own area, can be a great source of information. A manager's help is not only free, but unbiased, as he or she has your best interests at heart. Bank managers are in touch with the current business trends in the area, and know who is doing well and who isn't. They can tell you the general business climate of the area, if it's growing or declining, and where the major growth or expansion is taking place.

Lawyer
If your lawyer is located in the proposed area, then again, discuss the general business climate from his or her perspective.

Insurance Agent
By visiting one or two of the local insurance agents to discuss your insurance needs, you can gain a lot of valuable information as they are constantly traveling around within the business community and know if business is on the increase or decrease.

Local Business Associations
Again, membership growth or decline shows how healthy the business area is. These associations often produce annual reports, which detail the local area from a business point of view.

Local Government
Municipalities often produce reports on the area, detailing past growth patterns and future plans. They also have figures on the population mix, average incomes, ethnic groups within the area, and the types of dwellings.

Research Firms

They will basically provide the same information as the local governments, but at your request, they will limit their report to a specific area or radius within that area. If the local government is not producing regular reports on their municipality, it may be that the growth has stopped and that you are locating in a stagnant area.

Consultants

Consulting firms will carry out any of the above functions for you, and also all of the research listed in the things you can do. They should provide you with two alternatives:

1. A preliminary study of the general area, to ascertain if a restaurant is feasible.
2. A full feasibility study, geared to your particular restaurant and location.

The two important points here are that you know exactly what it will cost you and what the consulting firm will do for their fee.

Suppliers

Another good source of free information are the potential food suppliers you may use. The sales staff are in constant contact with other restaurants, and a discussion with one of their representatives could prove very beneficial. After all, you are a potential customer.

Shopping Malls

If you are locating in a shopping mall, the mall management have sales statistics for each year of their operation. And they often carry out their own surveys within the mall, to see where their customers come from, the frequency of visits, and the general age groupings.

If it is a new shopping mall, the owners should have conducted their own market studies of the area, and if they want you as a tenant, then you should have access to the information.

If you are planning to open a location in a shopping mall, there are certain differences from other locations. Very few people will visit a shopping mall just to eat in the fast-food area. The fast-food tenants live off the mall traffic, so if the mall does not have an attractive tenant mix to draw shoppers, you should question how well you are going to do.

You will also have to consider the commercial and residential area mix in which the shopping mall is located, the same way you would for any other location. For example, many downtown malls do an excellent lunchtime business, but very little on weekends or evenings. Any glowing reports or projections provided to you by the mall management will still have to be checked and verified.

Building the Customer Profile

Your operation's viability will depend on many factors, one of which is your customer profile. Who is your customer, and what do you know about him or her? All this must be decided and developed before you open.

1. Is your concept keyed to males or females?
2. Old or young guests?
3. Rich or poor? How much money will they need to visit you often?
4. Families or singles?
5. Food eaters or liquor drinkers? Or both?
6. Reservation business or walk-in trade?
7. Business people or casual diners?
8. Credit-card, expense-account trade?
9. Are you going to deliver items? Or pick-up/take-out trade?
10. How long will they spend on each visit?
11. Are there other traffic generators that will bring in your kind of customer?
12. How trendy are you going to be? And what will happen when you're not so trendy?

Hours of Operation

Your proposed hours of operation are also important. As the location you're now scouting is dependent upon many factors, the hours you are open will point out how your concept fits into the new area you're scouting.

1. Is your concept based on high volume?
2. Can you be open to allow for this high customer-count turnover?
3. Is your menu based on quick, ready-to-serve items to allow for this?

4. Or are you cooking to order for each request?
5. Will you be open early?
6. Is there enough customer traffic going past your location to make this okay?
7. At lunchtime, does the customer profile allow for half-or one-hour turns?
8. Will you be open late at night?
9. What kind of customers will visit then?
10. If you are basing your sales on dinner, is the area still populated at that time?
11. Or has everyone gone home? Such as in a city core? Or industrial park?
12. Are you going to be open every day of the week?
13. Does your lease allow you to be open seven days a week?
14. What days must you be closed according to state liquor laws?
15. Are you going to be open Sundays? If so, why?
16. Can you open on statutory holidays?
17. Is your concept based on customers that do not come into your area after dark?
18. Will other traffic generators be open when you are? Or closed?
19. When is your competition open? Why? Will you copy them? Why?

Case Study #2—Location

Dave and his brother-in-law Bob decided to get into the restaurant business, and they thought they knew what they wanted—an operation big enough for a stand-up bar and 125 seats or so. They figured they had enough money for the layout and decor changes, but not for the complete start-up costs. They were looking for a restaurant that had closed, so that they'd be able to buy all the chattels on a cut-rate basis. Both would be working in the operation.

When they began looking they couldn't find anything in their immediate area, a suburb, so they expanded the area of their search.

Bob called Dave one day about a location he'd found while driving around.

"It looks good, Dave," he said. "It's an old pizza place that went bankrupt almost a year ago, I hear. Let's check it out!"

So Bob and Dave started to scout the area. The restaurant had almost 4,000 square feet of usable customer space. That would give them the seating they needed, and still leave enough room for a stand-up bar. In fact, there was a perfect place for it, right against the kitchen wall. Its location would cost less than they'd budgeted for, because they wouldn't have to run the power and water lines a long way. The pizza ovens were of no use to them, they realized, so it would cost them extra to finish the equipment package they'd need to produce their menu.

All things considered, they decided the operation was perfect.

"But how about the location?" Dave asked. "Why did these guys go broke here?"

And so they began to research their immediate market area.

The restaurant was located on the ground floor of a small office building, on the corner of a residential and commercial area street.

In the immediate area were five other restaurants. Three were smaller sit-down-only shops, one of which served Italian cuisine, with real homemade pizza. That restaurant, open for almost ten years, had become part of the community, they realized.

Directly across the street from their location was a fast-food chicken outlet that they noticed did mostly a take-out trade. A Chinese-style outlet completed the food service available in the area.

"So no one will be doing our style of restaurant in the area," said Dave. "It still looks good."

Both Bob and Dave then ate at each restaurant in their area. Week after week they were in their competitors' dining rooms. They made sure to come at both lunch and dinner to see what kind of customer traffic they might be able to expect.

"Still looks good," said Dave, "and we should be able to generate more customers with our stand-up bar. There's both after-work and evening traffic too!"

Checking the local paper, they also found that the area had a local merchants' association which had compiled statistics on the area. Their copy of the report showed the area to be on the increase in traffic flow, customer counts, and sales volume.

Wandering around the area on his day off, Dave happened to talk to a carpet-store owner, who told him that his sales were up dramatically.

"And do you know why, Bob?" Dave asked. "Simple. There's a new high-rise that just started renting, a block away. And the superintendent said the whole building is made up of bachelor and one-bedroom apartments—just the kind of customers we need for the stand-up bar trade."

Because he'd been owed a few months back rent when the pizza place folded, the landlord, however, was a bit leery of re-renting to another restaurant. So now his lease included personal guarantees.

"But it's not that bad," Dave said. "We knew this attempt might cost us everything, so we'd better be right!"

"Right," Bob said. "So far we've got a new-style restaurant, in a growing area of both residential and commercial traffic, with enough local volume to succeed."

"Don't forget that new office tower going up, down the block, in six months. That'll be good for some more customers too."

"And there's a city parking lot behind our building, and the bus stop out front. So far so good. Let's do it!"

And they did, successfully!

Case Study #2—Critique

Dave and Bob approached their location search with one important criterion: that there was no rush. They would take all the time necessary.

1. They drove around their area, gradually moving outwards, and, in doing so, gained further knowledge of traffic patterns and the like.
2. Once they found what appeared to be the right location, they scouted the area, looking at the residential and commercial mix, as well as studying the competition.
3. They assembled an accurate customer profile and looked at where their customers would come from, how they would get there, and where they would park.
4. They fully explored the local papers, the city, and the trade association. They also talked to other retailers, as well as reviewed future developments planned for the area.

7

BUILDING YOUR DREAM

The project of developing a restaurant has no specific cost average that can be used as a guide for an individual or group to determine the expected construction costs. However, that is not to say that your project's expected costs cannot be budgeted for. A step-by-step guide for determining costs is presented later in this chapter.

The purpose of this section will be to outline areas important to an operation's birth.

Negotiating the Lease

When investigating a space it is important to investigate all costs associated with the space.

1. *Leaseholds* — site investigation
   — improvement costs
2. *Rental Terms* — cost per square foot
   — percentage rent
   — common-area expenses
   — advertising costs
   — taxes, real estate fees
   — business insurance
   — cost of utilities
   — up-front deposits and securities
3. *Improvements* — landlord allowances
   — landlord-performed work or improvements
   — any restrictions or limitations, whether for

design (because of product nature and/or local authorities), municipal, or other governing bodies.

4. *Rental Period* — length of lease
   — rights of renewal
   — landlord's rights
   — tenant's rights
5. *Legal* — lease documents: "The Standard Lease"
   — covenants: corporate and personal
6. *Area By-Laws* — approvals
   — release clause
   — restrictions

Leaseholds

Leaseholds involve the investigation of a site and the determination of improvements or improvement costs available from a landlord and the actual costs that present themselves when leasing space.

The major expenses for the development of a given site are incurred in the preparation of the site to receive the intended food operation. Many of these costs are nothing more than leasehold improvements. Major plumbing, electrical, mechanical, and construction material installations, which become immediately fixed to the building and are not removable by the tenant, are now the property of the landlord.

Rental Terms

Rental terms can be a combination of cost per square footage and percentage of earnings, or only one of the above. Do not be fooled by the quoted per-square-footage rent appearing cheap until all expenses have been accounted for as shown in the above outline.

Rental terms are not always set by the landlord and are negotiable despite what landlords would have you believe. The negotiation may include terms ensuring that the landlord provide all tenancy upgrading to meet the occupancy code for the space, and provide at least the required electrical power, mechanical heating, ventilation, and air conditioning system as determined by the tenant's designer and engineer.

Negotiations and the final signing of the lease may take considerable time and involve high legal costs. It is advisable to consult, even at this stage, with a selected design firm specializing in restaurant consultation. While the lawyer is skilled in leasing documents, phrasing, and interpretation, the designer is skilled in advising about specific location pitfalls and suggesting solutions. The design consultant can provide valuable information and assistance to your legal counsel in the assembly of your "offer to lease." Not all foodservice design consultants will participate in this area, and fees can vary greatly. Beware of personal covenants in leasing.

Improvements

Improvements of a retail space can be extensive, and the decision to locate in an area should not be based solely on how prepared the space might already be. It is more important to make your market study of a given area first, to determine if the area, concept, and clientele are favorable.

A favorable market study will indicate the expected potential of a given area. After you have determined the credibility of an area, investigate and establish, with the aid of your consultant, the power and services needed by the operation. This information and your design consultant's analysis of the retail area are critical to your bargaining for leasehold improvements.

Your design team can be very instrumental in advising and negotiating landlord conditions. Because the design team will have to work with conditions when a lease is finalized, it can, therefore, save considerable time and cost at this point. All local authorities and licensing bodies can be approached about tenancy use and to further check zoning and parking.

Rental Periods

Rental periods can, and do, vary sometimes at the express wish of the landlord to permit rental increases, and renewal options are often for shorter periods.

Because of the ever-increasing cost of land, development, property maintenance and upgrading, the landlord tries to reduce rental periods as much as possible. The same argument for increasing rental periods can be made by a restaurateur in so much as his initial development costs in preparing a given space to receive a restaurant, which are invisible to the finished product, are of a major proportion to the overall project.

Notwithstanding the size of a location, a minimum of a fixed fifteen-year period is desirable with two, five-year renewal options. Many landlords are reducing the length of leasing agreements, permitting rental increases dependent on the increased property values and rising mortgage costs. The greater the initial cost outlay, the greater the need for spreading the capital costs, and therefore the need for a fixed- or low-controlled rental fluctuation. When leasing, a sliding scale permitting rental cost escalation during the term of the leasing period can be predetermined.

It is important that all costs outlined under rental terms be clearly understood, since they, too, comprise part of the overall rental cost. A rental cost must be evaluated in direct association with sale projections, bank cost, loan repayments, operating costs, staff and utilities expenses, real and approximated. The restaurant owner's fiscal consultant can then advise on the acceptability of leasing costs in direct relation to the earning power of the location.

After all conditions of rental are completed the restaurateur should apprise himself of both the landlord's and tenant's rights under the leasing document. The documents generally favor the rights of the landlord/owner of the property.

Legal

Legal leasing documents are far from standard when dealing with a food operation (standard refers to document sections, not to the format of the conditions and schedules). While a lease is generally laid out in a rather common fashion, the many variables for food-service operations require expansion to incorporate the tenancy improvements by both the landlord and tenant.

Clear determination of all restrictions placed on the tenant should be fully worked out before signing—most specifically the determining of corporate and/or personal covenants.

Area By-Laws

Area by-laws are crucial. Never sign a lease without first having all required approvals and, if a lease is signed, be sure to include a release clause protecting against area by-law restrictions prohibiting the operation or effecting key identity factors.

Designing the Space

The Designer
The first step in designing your restaurant is to select the designer. Using the yellow pages or contacts with local trade or business associations will provide a list of qualified people within your area. But how do you assess their ability in foodservice design?

It may be more beneficial for you to visit operations in your area similar to what you are planning, and ask them who did the design work. Were they happy with the completed facility? Were there any problems with the designer? Were all the local requirements, by-laws, and codes met, or were there complications?

Once you have selected a short list of potential designers, meet with each one in an effort to determine what they will charge you for the project (fees and contracts are discussed later in this chapter), and ask for references from similar jobs they have completed. The main point you will want to clarify at this time is the comfort level you can establish with this individual. You will spend a great deal of time in designing and selecting the furnishings, equipment, fabrics and materials with the designer and, unless you can foresee a good working relationship, you had better look elsewhere, regardless of price and qualifications.

The Design

a. Defining the Requirements
There are certain prerequisites that the designer would expect you to have already established. The sort of menu, type of service and food determines the size of the kitchen, service and preparation area needs, storage and patron services (i.e., coatrooms, washrooms). It is important to understand that the mode of purchasing either desired or as dictated by local suppliers and accessibility will influence the storage and service areas. These factors have been pre-considered for the following example and an outline used originally to select the retail space and used in the leasing discussion is shown.

Example
For a 100-seat Italian restaurant (licensed) at 12 sq. ft. per person (optimal comfort level)—1200 square feet (seating area only). (This restaurant also has a take-out shop).

EXAMPLE

Our example is for a 100-seat Italian restaurant (licensed) with a take-out shop.

AREAS ACCESSIBLE TO CUSTOMERS
1. General Seating:
   12 sq. ft. per person × 100 persons   1,200 sq. ft.

2. Areas Not Included as Part of General Seating:

Service Bar	80 sq. ft.	
Vestibule	64 sq. ft.	
Lobby & Reception	70 sq. ft.	
Coatroom	64 sq. ft.	
Cashier	35 sq. ft.	
Service Stations	18 sq. ft.	
Amounts to approximately ¼ of seating area		331 sq. ft.

3. Public Washrooms:
   Minimum Space required   175 sq. ft.

4. Take-Out Shop:
   Minimum Space required—10 ft. × 15 ft.   150 sq. ft.

5. Display Cooking:
   Minimum Space required—9 ft. × 10 ft.   <u>90 sq. ft.</u>

         Total   1,946 sq. ft.

AREAS INACCESSIBLE TO CUSTOMERS
1. General Menu:
   Kitchen and service areas including space for: dish-washing; food preparation, cooking and storage; refrigeration and freezer; pantry; and drink-systems storage. Amounts to approximately ⅓ of the total space to which customers have access.   650 sq. ft.

2. Staff Washrooms:
   Minimum space required   <u>60 sq. ft.</u>

TOTAL AREA NEEDED   2,656 sq. ft.
    Ratio of unusuable space to the total is
    approximately 20%—corridors, aisles, etc.   <u>535 sq. ft.</u>

         Minimum Rental Space   3,191 sq. ft.

Using the example of the 100-seat Italian restaurant and given the foregoing, you can now begin to work out your own requirements with which to approach a designer.

b. Floor Plans

The difference between good and bad floor plans can be as minor as furniture positioning or as major as a poorly functioning kitchen operation.

A floor plan that is good for one operator may be unacceptable to another. The preparation and assembly of food, and the cooking and table service must be smooth, and professional, without staff overlap (the most desirable condition) or with limited overlap. Consideration must be given to the normal movement of traffic suited to the operation's nature, with regard to the public and functional areas (i.e., bar, dance floor, salad bar, waiting area, coatroom, etc.).

It is the client's job to detail the type of service and functional areas to be incorporated by the consultant. The consultant will provide space, time, and motion analysis of the operation and, through variables of a preliminary plan, assist the customer in evaluating a given area (*see* Samples 11 and 12).

c. Seating

There are a number of considerations to take into account for a seating layout.

1. Type of area (i.e., lounge, bar, restaurant, fast-food).
2. Type of seating.
3. Functional flexibility of seating.
4. Code applications, aisle sizing, service, and decorative finishes.
5. Table sizes and functional flexibilities.
6. Handicap requirements as applicable.

Seating is generally based on state or municipal code specifications, which can also greatly influence washroom services and the handicap facilities required, but the optimal comfort level is 12 square feet per person in the customer area.

Even after layout approval, seating is subject to variation. Actual space versus designed space can vary to allow more or less seating than specified—generally more seating is capable of being

SAMPLE #11

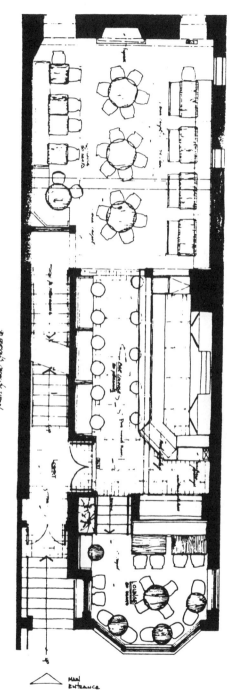

SAMPLE #12

installed. The consultant should advise the client of the recommended average to be considered when placing orders.

Table and chair sizing greatly affects the area. Larger chairs require slightly larger tables, but a minimum table size is required for licensed premises of 2 square feet per person. An example is a 24″ square, 2-seater table which is 4 sq. ft.—2 square feet per person. The consultant will advise the client of table size variations and shapes.

To maximize the seating capacity in a location, it is important to understand what functional seating is in a given operation. Tables and chairs that are positionally flexible can be relocated to accommodate groups or individuals. The seat capability in a restaurant is never fully realized. Approximately 80 percent of the seating is utilized, leaving 20 percent of the seating to be relocated or vacant. The reason for this is simple: too many larger-group tables or four-seater arrangements, too much booth seating which when used by small groups, couples, or individuals leaves vacant, unusable seating.

The consultant designs the layout to suit your function and style. He may not design for great flexibility if the restaurant is of a special nature. Remember that at this point, however, the required seating has been reflected and confirmed in accounting terms showing the turnover required to produce profitability. Should the seating count be restricted by inflexibility, the potential will not be reached.

Discuss fully the layout and furnishing sizes the consultant recommends to satisfy your needs. Understand costs in the development of the seating. Do not be fooled by quantity; that is to say, increased quantity of seating/tabling does not necessarily mean a cost increase. Finishing changes to manufacturers' catalogue items can create a cost increase or decrease. It is the consultant's function to advise and research sources on your behalf. Quantities of an increased nature often allow the supplier to offer quantity discounts, and finishing modifications can be negotiated. Shop wisely. Select for function, nature of design, and area compatibility. Obtain written confirmation of all prices, finishes, options (i.e., glides for carpet or tile areas), deliveries, discounts, and payment terms.

REMEMBER: EFFICIENCY BEFORE DESIGN, FUNCTION BEFORE LOOK!

Twenty Steps to Opening

It is extremely important that the client expresses likes and dislikes, cooking or operational preferences, and any specific direction desired in the project. Before any decorative considerations, the operational side and flow patterns must be established. Remember that *"form follows function."*

Step 1

The designer must first review the lease documents and visit the site to confirm all information and check all dimensions whenever possible.

Step 2

Equipment selection based on menu requirements.

Step 3

Preliminary study plans may involve a series of floor plans showing the many potential uses of the space and indicating the flow pattern for public and staff.

The preliminary floor plan shows kitchen, bar, and other services, and a general configuration of the area, but does not indicate, at this point, a design style or any finishing treatments.

Step 4

The selection and fine-tuning of the operational preliminary plan.

Step 5

Finalize equipment needs for menu and operators' methods. If staff (i.e., chef) is available some discussion should involve this individual. Never design a kitchen exclusively for one chef—the facility must work for any chef hired.

It is important for a client and consultant to relate openly and directly. The consultant must be aware of the client's ideas, method of operation, and any specific preferences for service.

Without the client's full trust and open discussion, the consultant is unable to fulfill his obligations satisfactorily. This stage is extremely critical to both the consultant and the client as the "working drawings" (final detailed design drawings) are developed from this stage.

Step 6

After equipment/operational plans are consolidated, the consultant will begin a like process to the operational planning by preparing conceptuals of the space. Conceptuals can take many forms:

1. Study sketches in black and white (*see* Samples 11 and 12).
2. Study sketches in color.
3. Preliminary freehand elevations/detail sketches.
4. Sample material assembly.
5. Field visits with or without the client to examine first-hand material installations, sources, or just to determine if a like product or material is available elsewhere.

It is important that an individual does not respond to materials or color on a personal level, but allows the consultant to marry the esthetic qualities with the operation. While the client should advise the consultant of particular dislikes the overall effect is important to a successful design.

The consultant should, however, take note of the feelings of the client and attend to such considerations. The mental attitude of the client towards a given concept can be important to the success of the project.

Step 7

Colored sample board and rendering(s).

Step 8

Full disclosure to the client of the design and materials prior to commencement of the working drawings.

Step 9

Working drawings, details, elevations, signage, graphics, equipment and specifications.

Step 10

Engineering—mechanical and electrical.

Step 11

All working drawings and specifications reviewed and cross-referenced.

Step 12

Apply for building permits and approvals from all governing authorities.

Step 13

Project tendered for bids on construction, equipment supply and installation.

Step 14

While tendering is under way (minimum two-week period), the client should be preparing menus for printing, selecting cash registers and equipment to coincide with construction completion. The client should further arrange for all utility services with the municipality.

Step 15

Tender review and examination. This review should be carried out with the designer/consultant's involvement and expertise. Usually this process can take from one to two weeks.

Step 16

Award of contract—signing of contract terms of payment. Commencement of construction, acknowledgment of consultant's role in the site's construction and finishing.

Step 17

Client begins hiring staff.

Step 18

Start-up and testing of equipment, staff training, trial runs. During this period trades will service the site to repair and adjust any problems that present themselves at this time.

Step 19

Unofficial opening and staff trials.

Step 20
Official opening.

The process for the design, development, and construction can take as long as twenty-six weeks, depending, of course, on the project size.

Case Study—Function versus Design

Harvey Brown was getting frustrated. For more than two hours he'd been refereeing between John, his designer, and Sam, his manager. And he'd barely been able to get a word in edgewise most of the time.

"Okay," said Harvey, "enough about the rug. Let's move on to the tables and chairs for the dining room."

Flipping through the furnishing spec book, John sought the right page. "Here they are. Okay now, they've already been decided on. The white wrought-iron chairs to match up with the ice-cream-parlor tables. With round 28" glass tops. Now let's move on."

"Just a minute," Sam said. "Wrought-iron chairs are heavy, aren't they?"

"About thirty-five pounds or so. Why?" John inquired.

"Because they may just be too heavy for the kids to move around at that weight," Sam replied.

"Never mind that," said John. "The parent always moves them around anyway."

"Okay," Sam agreed. "But how high are they?"

"The standard 27" height. Why?"

"And I suppose they have a round, padded seat, with no arms?"

"They're not supposed to have arms," John said, "The look we want is an old-time, ice-cream-parlor look, and that means no arms."

"Just why are arms important?" Harvey asked, happy to finally be able to contribute a question.

"Well," Sam said, "the kids will need a booster chair because those seats are too low for their normal dining height. And boosters will slide or fall off a chair without arms. It's just not . . ."

"Hold it," John interrupted. "We have to keep the look if the whole concept is going to succeed. Trust me, I've seen changes made that destroy . . ."

"Wait a minute, John, that's crazy. Are we going to give up function for design? And make the kids unsteady on their chairs and their mothers worried all through the meal?"

Harvey held up his hand and waited till they stopped arguing. "John," he said, "does the manufacturer make the same chair with arms?"

"Yes. But it's not within the concept, you know."

"But in line with function," Sam said.

"Okay, okay," Harvey said, "how much extra will it cost for chairs with arms?"

"If I can still get them on deadline, add about 20% to the cost of each chair. *If,* mind you!"

"Okay, start checking on it, please, John. Are the tables okay though?"

"Let me interrupt here," Sam said. "A round 28″ top doesn't give us enough room to set the table properly, and still leave enough room for the breadbasket, or wine glasses, or even side plates."

John snorted his reply. "There is more than enough room for that stuff. Besides, your servers are supposed to take that stuff away, so as not to clutter up the table, right."

"Only after it's been on the table first. The size and material just aren't right, Harvey."

"Oh, come on Sam, everyone used to use glass for table-tops," Harvey said. "Even I know that."

"Used to use it, right? But not now. We're expecting a high-volume restaurant, and you know how dirty a glass table-top will be after a group of kids gets finished with it. What are we sup-posed to do? Bring out the Windex and a no-lint cloth every time? It's just too much work and won't be done properly. We'll be seating guests at dirty tables."

"If you trained your staff better," John said, "It would get done right."

"And if you designers did a better job of designing functional operations, we'd have an easier time running them."

Harvey interrupted again. "Seems to me we'd better rethink both the tables and chairs."

"Oh, great," John said, "I thought these things were firmed up a month ago. Trying to change things now, if possible, might put the opening back awhile."

"But if it's not right, then we'll be saddled with the mistake forever. It must be right. Can you check on things, John?" Harvey said.

"I suppose we could hurry the manufacturer by paying a premium price for a rush order. It would be expensive. There's 270 chairs and 42 tables . . . but we'd make the opening."

"Expensive?" Harvey said. "Wait a minute here. What kind of a mess have I got myself into?"

Fee Structures and Contracts

The Professional Disciplines
Beyond the consultant's responsibility for the foodservice and interior design portion of the project, there are the mechanical/ electrical and structural design components or other such specialties necessary in the execution of the design of the project. Many consultants can provide this service using their recommended engineer(s) and specialists, or the client can hire these people independently.

It is wise to consider the specialists recommended by the consultant as these individuals have probably worked together on other projects and have formed an understanding and technique in the preparation of documents. The project will run more smoothly and be controlled by the design consultant, who acts as the project director for the client. The fees for such sources can be separated and paid directly to the appropriate person or through the consultant. When paid through the consultant, it is not unusual for some consultants to mark up the fee. Most consultants, however, allow for the cost of project direction in their fee structure and have the individuals contract directly with the client.

The client who hires professionals who are not skilled in this specific kind of project, or not holding the required building department accreditation, can suffer, if not financially, then operationally. (Refer to the section following for professional services' fees and contracts.)

Most projects require only the design/foodservice consultant and electrical/mechanical engineers. In certain projects, however, it is necessary to involve other specialists. Before contracts are issued, the consultant should assemble this group of specialists, and outline fees for follow-up by the client.

The following specialists may be called upon in a project:

1. Designer/Foodservice Consultant
2. Electrical Engineer
3. Mechanical Engineer
4. Structural Engineer
5. Site Survey Engineer (if no survey can be provided)
6. Graphic Specialist
7. Sign Specialist

The designer/consultant generally takes care of the following areas, which may or may not require a separate contract:

1. Sound systems
2. Lighting special effects
3. Specialty equipment

In some cases the design consultant and foodservice consultant are two different people. There are specialists who are both design and foodservice oriented and who specialize strictly in all forms of foodservice or food-related design projects.

When selecting the consultant, be sure that you feel comfortable with him or her. The consultant should be open and direct, and you should review his or her capabilities and experience.

Fees and Contracts

The success of a company depends on good business practices and professional ethics. As each project varies in scope, the pertinent professionals should review all details of fees with the client before proceeding with any work, and clearly outline the schedules and options available within the scale recommended by various professional bodies and standard practices. Professionals often vary their methods of charging fees, based on the type of work being done, as follows:

1. *Fixed Fee* on all or any section of the work for:
   — Design studies
   — Contract drawings and specifications
   — Assistance in calling tenders
   — Casual supervision or field supervision (not to be confused with the management of construction done by a contractor)
2. *Hourly Rates* for all or any section of the work based upon an estimated total cost of service.
3. *Percentage Fee* on a selected piece of work by prior agreement.

Fee costs as fixed fee and percentage fee rates are on a sliding scale and are peculiar to the given project conditions and costs. Each specialist can provide a written confirmation of the services being provided for the fee. Because of the nature of the product, contracts are generally written to suit each client. Read and understand the contract and terminology expressed. If the terminology gives the impression of more than one approach, have the document altered so that it is specific and clear in meaning.

Construction

Construction Contracts
Most contracts fall short of the desired requirements and conditions of a given project. With the burden of extensive landlord demands and banking practices placed on today's entrepreneur, it is risky, at best, to trust unproven agreement vehicles. As an individual would select a consultant, so should the contract document be selected—maximum control based on a proven track record. This form of contract gives the consultant some teeth, so the job is done right.

Failure to complete work, a bankruptcy, the non-payment of a subtrade or even the failure to pay taxes, duties, insurances, or even Workmen's Compensation costs—all these things occur far too often. The client is vulnerable legally and personally under different circumstances in the event of any of these events occurring. Place the burden and responsibility in the proper place before commencing construction by insisting on a proper contract form. Protect yourself: examine and discuss with your consultant the different forms of agreement.

a. Created Documents
This form of agreement is a creation by the contractor and, in many instances, is general in nature. This form is more generally seen for small, short-term projects. While suggesting a complete contract, and listing and attaching the contract drawings and specifications, these agreements are not sufficiently binding. They are binding for what is documented but what about permit and inspection fees, client indemnification, and workers' compensation costs? Are you to assume you are safe? Don't assume!

Review the document carefully, and add to it, in black and white, all verbal assurances made. Most importantly (before signing), have your lawyer review all legal documents.

Construction Supervision
Construction supervision can be carried out in one of two ways:

1. General Construction Contract
2. Project Management Contract

a. *General Construction Contract*
The general contractor provides constant, on-site supervision and control for projects of a size dictating the attention. Smaller projects generally would have a working supervisor to coordinate the productivity while at the same time performing a particular construction function.

The supervisor on the large site is kept extremely busy documenting trade schedules, work control, directing day-to-day trade interaction, receiving materials, etc. The supervisor may or may not take part in actual manual creation on-site.

b. *Project Management Contract*
When constructing a project with a project management contract, the trades are all paid for by the client directly, but the management firm provides a knowledgeable supervisor who acts on the client's behalf on-site in much the same fashion as a general contractor supervisor. The management firm receives a fee for the following services rendered:

1. Review all trades/contracts.
2. Administer contracts.
3. Coordinate schedule of project work.
4. Review all payments, progress draws, issuing appropriate documentation or obtaining same before releasing approval for payment.
5. Ensure draw payments correspond to work complete or on-site and again obtain certificates of compliance to void lien action, etc.
6. Prepare reports, chair site meetings with client and design specialists.
7. Criticisms, revisions, alterations, cancellations, deletions, and/or rejection of work is directed through this individual for sub-trades.
8. Final site inspection with design specialists.

c. *Client-Trade Relation*
An owner/client should refrain from open criticism or comments to the trades. All discussion regarding site conditions are to be discussed with the site supervisor, no matter how the project is being controlled. Unless the client is experienced in site-development scheduling, it is possible to be misinterpreted when making casual comments or discussing site progress with a sub-tradesman. This direct contact spoils the supervisory control and can, at times, lead to extras. Tradesmen look for short cuts, not an uncommon practice in any business, but on a project dependent on rigid construction permits, code requirements, time schedules and cost controls, even a simple variation can cause a delay and affect costs. The complaint, question, or pat on the back should be directed to the site supervisor, who is in a better position to look after the client's interests.

Other Regulatory Agencies
The following list of municipal, local, and other governing bodies should be consulted when building on a location. The need to see these parties varies among municipalities. Additional requirements, peculiar to a given area, may present themselves at the time of permit application. To avoid embarrassment, it is worthwhile to develop a basic preliminary plan for the intended retail area, and take it along when discussing your proposal with the

different controlling bodies. By doing this, you will be able to get their reactions to the planned establishment and to learn of any objections they might have.

Applications for building permits should be made for all of the following, if applicable to your project:

1. Construction
2. Mechanical
3. Electrical
4. Plumbing
5. Demolition
6. Drainage
7. Sign permit
8. Zoning (for proper area designation, parking etc.)
9. Exterior building design variations (planning department of the local or state authorities will rule on special variances)
10. Fire safety regulations and requirements (Fire Department)
11. Engineering

The following regulatory bodies may also have to be consulted:

1. Labor department
2. Health department
3. Local or state authorities regarding liquor licensing (where applicable)
4. Environmental Protection Agency (as applicable for exhaust odors, etc.)
5. Local or state authorities regarding signage on Highways
6. Local historic society board (special approvals for historic sites)
7. Local power company (special service upgrading, i.e., transformers)
8. Consumers gas (new gas services)
9. Department of public works (new sewer and water services on public property and connection to city services as applicable) (*see* Chapter 10)

Equipment and Furnishings

Once you have decided upon your concept and menu style of service, the next step in planning your sit-down restaurant is to consider the equipment and furnishings you will need.

The most important thing to remember is efficiency. It is this single factor that will determine how smoothly your restaurant operates. Making mistakes in the initial planning and buying of equipment will mean constant problems later on. Pick the wrong equipment, and your service and quality will suffer. And the customers notice that immediately.

Complementing your original concept is your menu. This is the single most important criterion in deciding upon the equipment needed to produce that menu. If you are not knowledgeable in selecting the equipment to produce certain menu items, get help. Your designer, in conjunction with your kitchen equipment company, will be able to supply a range of prices and models for the same pieces of equipment. Do not overlook their advice concerning the reliability of such equipment and information regarding maintenance and repair.

Let's begin by looking into your own restaurant. Traditionally, the industry has split a restaurant into two separate areas: the back and the front of the house.

Back of the House

This is most easily defined as all the areas that are usually hidden from the customers' view and inaccessible to them. Generally, they include the kitchen, behind the bar, offices, storage areas, staff rooms, etc. Usually, they are decorated in an entirely different manner and style than the areas the customer sees.

They get heavy, messy use and with sanitation and cleanliness in mind, floors and walls are often tiled, according to the Board of Health Standards. Fire regulations also impose strict standards on materials used for these areas. Your designer will be responsible for applying the correct codes and standards in planning these surfaces.

Your menu will be used to determine which pieces of equipment you need in the kitchen. There are many types of cooking equipment available on the market. Be selective, but listen to the designer's advice.

a. Line Equipment

The line in the kitchen is the actual cooking bank of equipment lined up to produce all menu items. This line can be composed of many different pieces of equipment to produce varied menu items.

Different types of restaurants require different equipment. Some examples found on the line are as follows:

1. Ovens—often with flat-top griddles, or flame-top burners.
2. Salamanders—used to finish or brown food items.
3. Griddles—used to cook eggs, bacon, pancakes, etc.
4. Broilers—used to broil steaks, burgers, ribs, etc.
5. Fryers—used to deep-fry potatoes, breaded, or battered food items.
6. Fryers—used to deep-fry fish products.
7. Warming stations—used to hold food just before plating.
8. Woks—used to stir-fry Chinese food or fresh vegetables.
9. Convection Ovens—used to quick-bake volume products.
10. Steamers—used to steam food under pressure.
11. Steam Kettles—used to produce large-volume liquid foods such as soup.
12. Toasters—used to toast products.
13. Pizza Ovens—to produce pizza, of course.
14. Pasta Cookers—to cook large volumes of spaghetti, linguini, etc.

This is just a partial list of all the equipment that may be needed to produce your menu. Many items have multiple uses which can be a big moneysaver in your equipment budget. These line equipment items are in a line, against a specially-built firewall. Their placement is of the utmost importance. Improper placement means your line cooks will be crossing over in front of each other to produce food items. This causes inefficient cooking, lost time, and costly waste. Nothing contributes more to kitchen inefficiency than incorrect placement of equipment along the line. During operation of the line, each line cook mans his own station, and performs certain tasks in cooking your menu items. Crossover during a lunch or dinner-hour rush will mean total chaos behind the line. All wasted menu items will drastically affect your food cost and the service to your customers. The wrong placement of equipment will be a problem you will have to live with every day you're open, so have it designed correctly by an expert!

b. Construct and Plating Tabling

This row of equipment and tabling stands opposite the line equipment in a mirror image of usage. It is composed of steam table, cold tables, microwave ovens, under-table refrigeration, and storage. Above this table, sit overshelves, with your chosen plating on it, such as actual plates, baskets, steak boards, etc.

Below-table refrigeration will hold all menu items that have been fully prepared. That is, they are now ready to cook per order, having already been bought, refrigerated, cleaned, portioned and re-refrigerated. All a line cook has to do is take out a steak, burger, etc., and put it directly onto the broiler behind him. That is why placement of the tabling is important too. It must be correct, so that the line cooks do not have to cross over again.

Steam tables may hold everything from today's special, vegetable of the day, roast beef to slice, mashed potatoes, sauces, soups, etc.

Cold tables generally hold all the cold items ready to construct menu items: lettuce, pre-sliced meats for cold sandwiches, dressings, fresh vegetables, cheeses, eggs, sauces, tuna salad, etc. These items are also fully prepared, and held refrigerated to prepare to order.

In the production of any menu item, careful coordination between the line cooks will result in perfect production of that item. And that successful production is based on proper placement of all equipment to cut down on crossover and resulting chaos and waste.

c. Food Storage and Equipment
Food bought by your operation will always be stored away after receiving and checking. Equipment used for this may range from large walk-in refrigerators and freezers to smaller reach-in coolers, dessert coolers, dairy coolers, etc. Your designer will again work in conjunction with your kitchen equipment company in recommending the necessary equipment based on your sales volume projections. This is to ensure that you don't run out of product. Dry storage is used to store all canned, pailed, and bottled food products that do not need refrigeration before they are opened. They are usually kept in a large, multi-shelved room for inventory control.

d. Preparation Equipment
Generally, restaurants use all kinds of equipment to prepare food items. Food products are bought in their natural state and delivered to you according to your specifications. When the prod-

ucts come in your back door, they have to be prepared for your use. This may entail many procedures before they are ready to cook.

Equipment used for preparation saves many man-hours in labor, and generally makes for a uniform product. Some examples of preparation equipment are: slicers, mixers, blenders, choppers, etc. They are used to produce each menu item, ready to cook-to-order, by your line cooks. Here again, your designer and kitchen equipment company will recommend equipment based on the volume of product they can produce.

e. Sanitation
Once the customers have finished their meals, their plates and cutlery must be washed, as well as all the cookware used to produce and prepare their meals.

There are all kinds of dishwashers available, and most do a good job. Remember that your sales forecasting will establish a volume of food business and that volume will determine the necessary capacity of your dishwasher. Extensive stainless-steel tabling is generally included in the package to ease clean-up.

f. Kitchen Cookware
This package generally includes all of the pots, pans, bowls, whips, ladles, frypans, racks, trays, bus pans, pails, collanders, tongs, lids, inserts, etc. Your kitchen equipment company will advise you on their number and cost. The package can be expensive as it contains stainless steel and cast-aluminum materials, but their durability is usually excellent.

In general, the back-of-the-house equipment is expensive, varied, and critical. Listen to your designer and kitchen equipment company's advice. In the long run they will save you money. They are your "experts", and you are paying them for that advice.

Front of the House
The areas that customers have access to are generally defined as the front of the house. They can include the dining room, bar, washrooms, etc. These areas receive heavy traffic, as your sales forecasting has already shown you, so all the materials used in this area of construction must be of heavy-duty quality. Your designer will again have to specify certain rugs, wallcoverings,

ceiling tiles, paint, exposed wood, etc., that meet Board of Health and fire regulations. Some municipalities also have additions to the building code that are even stricter in their specifications. Again, your designer must be familiar with them.

a. Layout

Working with your designer, you must first okay the layout designs based on your concept. Preliminary discussions with him will be of great value in ensuring that your concept is enhanced by the layout of the restaurant. The layout is not only planned around the seating and bar, but is also flow-charted to ensure maximum efficiency. The designer will do this for you, to aid in the service of food and beverages within the restaurant. Flow-charting is not difficult, but should be done by an expert. This is very important for the operation of a smoothly-run restaurant. Make a mistake in layout and the result will be a confused pattern of customer and staff traffic.

b. Tables and Chairs

Picking the furnishings for the restaurant can be a long and involved process. Everything must be taken into consideration. First, it is important to qualify each item by its function. Your designer will recommend tables and chairs or booths. Are they functional? Of the correct size? Or weight? Do they compliment the concept? Are they of commercial quality, able to withstand restaurant wear-and-tear? Guaranteed? What finishes are used, and will they clean up well? And, finally, how much are they?

c. Decor

Using your concept, your designer will suggest different types of decor for the walls whether they be painted, paneled or papered. This might include paintings, murals, old nostalgic signs, menu boards, etc. These are important items as they create a pleasant, enjoyable atmosphere that will bring customers back.

Many restaurants now use plants to create this atmosphere, but they can be very costly. Live plants need maintenance on a regular basis. There are even leasing companies now that will provide plants to your specifications and come in regularly to maintain them, all for one monthly payment. They even replace the dying ones that have trouble adapting to the restaurant atmosphere of changing humidity, temperature, smokiness, etc.

d. Sound System

Most restaurants have a built-in sound system to provide background music for their customers. This may take many forms, from loud rock 'n roll for the singles bars, to muzak piped in quietly. The loudness of the music depends on your concept, but customers are very quick to notice poor sound, no matter what the volume levels, so it pays to buy a quality system.

e. Cash Control Systems

There are many types of systems available for the prospective restaurateur to choose from. After deciding upon the method for collecting money for meals and drinks, based on the system for issuing these items, you must choose a cash register. Get in touch with the companies specializing in their sale and maintenance. They will provide complete demonstrations of their systems before you commit yourself to buying one. Talk to other restaurants about the same equipment, and find out about its performance. Ask the waitresses how they like the machine. Learn as much as you can about all the systems before you decide. Although these machines are costly, you may be able to lease the unit before you open. Again, study what's available.

f. Security Systems

At any one time, your restaurant may have tens of thousands of dollars in inventory on hand, and a safe full of receipts. Protect those assets by having an alarm system installed before you open. Restaurants are robbed all the time, generally through the break-and-enter type of robbery. Even if the thieves can't get into your safe, they'll steal food and liquor, and vandalize the restaurant. You may be insured for some losses, but cleaning up the mess may cost you a few days' business. So protect your investment.

g. Smallwares

Again this package must fit into your chosen concept. Smallwares generally refer to the kind and style of plating, cutlery, basketware, glassware, table tops, napkins, etc. Your kitchen equipment company will provide complete breakdowns on prices of these items.

Your restaurant will also need an ice machine for both beverage service and kitchen needs. Some restaurants also have a salad bar, which requires a lot of ice daily. These units are very touchy pieces of equipment, and need service often. The placement is of great importance to ensure that ice can be taken from it easily without interrupting the normal work flow of your employees.

There are hundreds of suppliers of these items varying in price and quality. Choose the right kind for your operation by consulting with the designer. The concept you have chosen must be complemented throughout the restaurant, and the smallware package is very important. These items will be handled by every single one of your customers. They will often judge your restaurant by the smallwares' quality and cleanliness. Make sure you check on re-order prices of these goods. Many companies price the initial purchase price lower than the replacement cost. Be prepared for this in advance. Also check on delivery times for the package. Is the item coming from overseas or just across the state?

h. Bar Systems

The design and plan of the bar in your licensed restaurant, whether service or stand-up, is another very important fact. Customers want prompt service from a bar. Your designer will provide recommendations concerning the necessary equipment to allow for that service. A glass washer, back-bar, cooler, auto-bar, and cocktail units are just some of the necessary pieces you might need. You will also have to decide upon the decor for a stand-up bar, because its atmosphere will attract customers to you.

Equipment placing for the bar should also be flow-charted to allow for maximum efficiency, as most bars are small in size. The use of an auto-bar is suggested because it will save on the beverage costs and controls necessary when dealing with liquor and staff. Again, your designer will have to observe health and fire codes in the bar's construction.

Terms and Delivery

There are still two major points to consider before concluding this section. Because you will be spending thousands of dollars on equipment and furnishings, you and your designer need to be concerned with the following, in dealing with the suppliers of these items.

a. Terms
You should ask the suppliers the following questions about their terms:

1. What terms of payment are expected by the suppliers?
2. Do you have to put a deposit on the order?
3. When is the balance due?
4. What about returning substandard goods?
5. Is there a guarantee?
6. Is there a cancellation charge?
7. Is there a rush-order charge?
8. Is there a custom-made charge?

b. Delivery
Your goods are expected and coordinated to be delivered on a certain day. Timing is most important in a restaurant opening. The failure to appear of just one item may often delay an opening by days or weeks. And delays cost big money. So make sure each supplier can handle the order you place with him. Check his reputation and track record with other customers. Can he supply what you've ordered at the right price and on time? What if he can't? Have you an alternate supplier in case he goes broke, has a fire, etc.?

c. Foodservice Equipment Contract
This contract is generally a conditional sales agreement. Such an agreement should list all equipment with serial numbers and costs and should be dated and signed.

   Some foodservice equipment contractors register the contract retaining title of same until full payment is made under the contract. There is no formal structured agreement for this portion of the work due to the constant variations possible.

Used Equipment
Before purchasing used equipment of any kind, discuss your ideas with the design consultant.

Used equipment is obtained in one of four ways:

1. Bankruptcy Sale
2. Public Auction
3. Trade-in
4. New goods sold and reclaimed due to non-payment of account.

To affect a profit of any kind, the used equipment dealer must transport the goods to his shop, clean, repair, and refinish and then sell the item for as much as 80 percent of its original value. Depending on the age and condition of the item, a 90-day warranty is provided. If no repairs are made apart from a quick clean-up, it might be sold in an as-is condition for cash-and-carry terms.

Many banks will restrict financing on used equipment and many landlords include in their leases a clause allowing only new and approved equipment to be installed.

Used equipment may appear to be cheaper than new equipment, but if you have to start changing the design of your restaurant to accommodate your bargain buys, or if substitutions effectively weaken the strength of your kitchen, then the net result could be higher construction costs and higher labor costs as a result of kitchen inefficiency.

Other Start-Up Considerations

No discussion on building, buying, or franchising a restaurant would be complete without mentioning some of the other start-up cost factors you may incur. Because some of the items listed below, such as uniforms and printing, have to be completed and ordered several weeks prior to your planned opening, sufficient lead-time and capital must be allowed for these areas.

Uniforms
Many manufactures stock popular styles of uniforms, if this fills your requirements. But if your concept calls for a unique design or unusual materials, than a minimum of eight weeks should be allowed.

Printing and Graphics

Again, a good lead-time may be necessary, especially if you require specific or unusual art work, logos or designs for your menus or placemats. You may also wish to consider using other printed items, such as matches, guest check, napkins, and stationery.

Utilities

Power and possibly heating will have to be made available during construction, and this may be your responsibility. Apart from the cost of energy used, the utility companies may require a deposit which they will hold for as long as you are in operation at your premises.

Insurance

Your insurance obligations will start the moment you take possession of the premises. Apart from your general needs (*see* Chapter 10), once in operation, it may be necessary, or prudent, to have insurance coverage during construction, especially to cover you against tradesmens' liability and vandalism.

Pre-opening Salaries

If your operation calls for key experienced staff, manager, chef, etc., you may hire these individuals some weeks before opening. All other staffing requirements will have to be filled before opening to allow for clean-up, organization, training, and dry-runs.

Inventory

Before opening, all food, liquor, paper, and cleaning requirements will have to be purchased. As a new operator, credit facilities may not be available until you have established your business (*see* Chapter 14).

Advertising

You may wish to advertise, or book advertising, before opening, or have signage prepared to inform the public of your opening.

Cash Float

Your operation will need a cash float in order to make change for customers, or to meet any C.O.D. deliveries.

Cost Overruns

Whatever your budget figure is for the total restaurant package, you should always allow 10 percent to 15 percent for cost overruns, due to price increases or delays.

Working Capital

There is no guarantee that your restaurant will make money from day one. In fact you may lose money for the first few months, or, at best, break even. So allow for this expense.

And remember, most of the experts, contractors, and suppliers you have used prior to opening will expect most, if not all, of their monies on completion of their work, so don't expect to meet the balance of these payments out of the first month's sales.

8

BUYING YOUR DREAM

It is a commonly held belief that the only businesses for sale are the ones that are losing money, or at best, breaking even. Although this may be true in many instances, it is not the only reason why a business may be up for sale.

Consider what happens to an operation when the owner/operator dies and there is no one in the family who is willing or capable of taking over. The same situation can arise because of illness or a permanent health problem, or the owner may want to retire and decides to sell his restaurant and live on the proceeds.

Another common situation in our present society is a marriage breakdown and divorce between a husband and wife who own and operate a business. As they are often partners in the business, the only agreeable recourse left to settle their affairs is to sell the business.

The situation can also arise where a person who is an absentee owner, with other business interests, simply wishes to put his money to other uses. Or sometimes a partnership breakdown can arise when silent or active partners simply cannot work together anymore.

As you can see, there are genuine reasons for a profitable restaurant to come onto the market. But be warned, it is up to you to verify whether or not the reasons given for the sale are true.

How to Find a Restaurant for Sale

Real Estate Companies
Only approach real estate companies that specialize in restaurants and commercial properties. Remember that the agent is working

for the vendor. Because he makes his living from selling, his advice could be biased.

This may not be the first time an agent is selling the same business. Ask him why the vendor is selling, and see if his answer matches that of the owner and staff.

Newspapers and Magazines

Business sections of all newspapers and certain trade magazines advertise restaurants for sale. If the sale is not going through a real-estate agent, the vendor may be willing to accept a lower price because there are no commissions to pay.

Word-of-Mouth

Friends and relatives who know you are looking for a business, business associates, or people you know in the trade can often provide information on restaurants that are for sale. Your accountant, lawyer or bank manager may have a client who wants to sell his business.

Scouting

Just by driving around your area, you may see restaurants for sale. If you see a location that looks perfect for your particular business, and it is not for sale, don't be afraid to go in and ask the owner (never the staff) if he has considered selling his business. You might get lucky.

Restaurant Open—Points to Consider

The approach to scouting an operation that is open is generally straightforward, on the whole. There is nothing wrong with scouting each location you are interested in by appearing as a customer, on a day-to-day basis. You are interested in the operation of the restaurant and the best way to judge whether it is suitable for your needs is to be in it when it is open. Much of the information you will be compiling should be written down—never trust your memory. You may wish to conceal the fact that you are taking notes on the operation. This can be done by referring to the classified section of the daily paper, open on your table or the bar. Simply pretend to be looking for an apartment, circle some listings beforehand and make notes constantly in the margins. Remember to take the paper with you when you leave and assemble the notes at home.

Customer Traffic

Consider the following points when assessing customer traffic:

1. Visit the restaurant at all times of the day.
2. Stay for the lunch and dinner rush, as a customer.
3. Take a count of customers coming in for meals.
4. Do they have a rush? Which days? What times?
5. What kind of customers are they? Categorize by age, sex, business type (professional or blue collar), reasons for frequenting the restaurant (business, pleasure).
6. Are they eating and drinking?
7. How many are in the average party?
8. How much turnover is there at mealtimes?
9. Can you generate an estimate of the size of the average guest check to reach a sales-volume total?
10. Are many customers walk-ins (i.e., unplanned visitors)
11. Is there a late-night trade?

Restaurant Details

Check the following details when scouting a restaurant:

1. What is the layout of the restaurant?
2. How many seats are there? Is there a bar?
3. How many seats is the restaurant licensed for?
4. How many employees are on duty during the day? And at what times for rushes?
5. How are the employees dressed? And how is their attitude and appearance?
6. What style of service is being used? How is the quality?
7. Check the menu style and pricing. Is there take-out?
8. Check the tabletops, kind of plating and cutlery in use, based on service generally.
9. Who manages the restaurant? Is the owner present?
10. What controls do they have on food and beverage items? Can the system be beaten?
11. Is there common-area seating? How is it maintained?
12. Of what quality are the furnishings? How have they stood up to wear-and-tear? Are they being maintained?
13. Does the music and the lighting complement the restaurant?
14. What sort of information will the staff give you about the operation? Often the staff is the best source of information.

Location Analysis
The following questions should be asked when analyzing the location:

1. Where is the parking for the restaurant?
2. What is the feeling about the operation within the area?
3. Are there complaints about its service or quality?
4. How much advertising does it do? Where? When?
5. Does it have a good community image?
6. What hours and days is it open?
7. What is the competition? And how are their sales?
8. Is the area increasing in growth? Decreasing?
9. Are there new developments coming? Changes?

Case Study—Believing the Thief

Murray White wanted to buy his own restaurant and after looking for quite a while, he thought he'd found the right one. It was a fast-food taco outlet in a large shopping mall, surrounded by more than 80 stores and with acres of parking. It was a busy, established mall, and the food court had over 250 chairs for diners.

Murray had received the last year's profit-and-loss sheet from the real estate agent handling the sale. It showed sales of $210,000 for the past 12 months. On those sales, he'd seen that the food cost of the operation had leveled out at 38 percent overall, a percentage he felt was high for that type of operation. Yet labor on the other hand was only at 22 percent, including the owner/manager's salary. Something was not quite right, Murray felt, but the real estate agent was unable to explain it.

So Murray sat down with the owner and asked all the right questions. The owner was very candid when he explained the discrepancies.

"It's simple, really. I haven't been reporting all my sales. What I do is try to take about $300 off the top for my pocket. That way, I only have to draw $12,000 salary and it keeps my labor cost down. It does raise my food cost, because the skim had to show up somewhere. And because I'm on a percentage rent, it keeps that down, too. No sense giving it all away in taxes anyways, right?"

Murray agreed at first but later he began to think about it. It just didn't sound right. After all, it was theft, no matter how you looked at it. Checking with the mall management company he discovered that the owner had reported $210,000 in sales, and at 8 percent rent it came to $16,800. If he had stolen $300 a week for 52 weeks, that was $15,600, and a saving of $1,250 on the rent.

So Murray went ahead and bought the restaurant, thinking that $15,600 and a saving of $1,250 looked better in his pocket than the old owner's. And he began to run his new taco restaurant.

It was only two weeks later that Murray knew he'd been had. The man had simply lied to him. Sales were only what they'd appeared to be on the profit and loss statement, and there wasn't any $300 to pocket weekly.

He'd been so mesmerized by the thought of $15,000 tax-free that he'd overlooked some things. If he'd checked more carefully, he would have noticed that the main reason for the high food cost was the untrained staff. They constantly ruined food and there was a lot of waste.

And the low labor cost? Sure the old owner only took home $12,000 annually, but he had his wife working there on an hourly rate. And she had made almost $15,000 in the last year.

Murray's biggest mistake, as he sadly realized, was believing the thief. He'd been so excited by the mythical $15,000 that he'd quickly agreed to pay the full asking price for the restaurant. Thinking that he'd better jump on the deal before someone else did, he hadn't even bothered to negotiate the price.

Restaurant Closed—Points to Consider

When scouting a restaurant that is closed, the most important question to ask yourself is why? Why is it closed? What factors contributed to its demise? And are you planning to employ any of those same factors in your operation?

Location and Style

1. Was it in the wrong location?
2. Is it in a saturated market?
3. What was the competition like?

4. Study the area again completely with respect to traffic flow, parking, residential and commercial areas, competition, and growth patterns.

Previous Owner

1. Did he run his own restaurant?
2. Was there a manager?
3. What happened? and why?
4. What information can the landlord provide?
5. What other businesses are in the area?
6. How good were the owner's systems and controls?
7. What paperwork is still on hand?
8. Who actually has control of the restaurant or its assets?

Previous Menu

1. What kind of menu was in use?
2. What pricing?
3. How did that fit into the area?
4. What about the competition's menus and pricing?
5. How did the menu reflect on service within the restaurant?
6. What equipment is in place to produce that menu?
7. Is it of use to you with your menu?
8. Much of an operation is keyed to the menu it must produce. Can you adapt the operation to your menu?

Pricing Structure

1. Were the prices out of line for the area?
2. Was the quality of food not up to par?
3. What was the feeling in the area about the prices?
4. Were they milking the area?
5. How many price increases did they have and when?

Assessing the Value

Before making an offer on any closed restaurant you must satisfy yourself on its value to you! Because the operation is closed, there is no goodwill included in the purchase price. What you are buying is the assets of the operation—the equipment, furnishings, fixtures and the lease.

Begin by doing a complete appraisal of all equipment and furnishings throughout the restaurant. If you can't assess the value of a piece of equipment, have an expert come in and do the appraisal for you. It will cost you some money, but it will be worth it. As well as giving you a total value of the operations package, he will also give you the value of individual pieces of equipment so you will have some idea of their worth. This will be helpful as he will also tell you if they are worth anything on the used market if you have no need for them in your planned operation. Watch out for rented equipment still on-site.

Once you have an appraised value of the contents, you have the value, to you, of the operation. Nothing else should be considered as part of what you are buying. Make sure you discount those items which have been leased; they are not for sale. You may be able to renegotiate with the owners for re-leasing them. But they may decline; many leasing companies have been stung too often by restaurants going broke. You may have to buy new equipment to replace these items.

Next consider renovations throughout the operation. With your menu and style of service, what will you have to do to change the present layout and equipment to conform with your concept and design? Where will power and water come from for new equipment? How much will it cost to build in a salad bar or new booth seating? What about new rugs, ceiling tiles, paint, or wallpaper? Has there been any damage due to the restaurant being closed for a while? Again, get experts to give you quotes on the cost of renovating. You will need a firm idea of the renovations necessary and how much they will cost in total.

Finally, consider the potential of the operation to you. You have already spent time on your concept and location analysis. Can this location be adapted to your use successfully? Can you afford it? With your new operation in place, does it have the potential of being successful? Can you see yourself in that operation, with your concept?

Making the Decision

Now that you have gathered as much information as possible, you will have to make a decision. A review of the major points may help in this regard.

The Reason

1. Why is the location for sale, and is the reason given, valid?
2. What is the asking price and how flexible is that price?
3. What is the location worth to you, considering changes, renovations, additional equipment, and furnishing?
4. Is there an audited or unaudited statement available for the location, and if not, why not?
5. If the answer to #4 above, is that the present owner did not report all the sales, can you believe this fact?
6. How long has the present owner operated the location, and how often has the location changed hands and why?

The Lease

1. What is the length of the lease?
2. Are there any renewable periods, and is this fact in writing?
3. Is the rental term fixed, or does it escalate?
4. Are there any special conditions in the lease which could affect your business?
5. Do you have to pay percentage rent on top of base rent?
6. Are you on the head lease (a tenant of the landlord) or on a sublease (tenant of the seller).
7. Does the leasing arrangement affect your ability to sell or franchise this location?
8. Has your lawyer reviewed the lease with you?

Before the Offer Is Made

1. If the offer is drawn up by the real estate company, let your lawyer establish that you are fully protected, before you sign.
2. Do you have a list of chattels (equipment, furniture, etc.), and have you checked it thoroughly against what is actually on the premises?
3. Any equipment that is not on the list of chattels may be loaned or hired to the restaurant. Can you make the same arrangement?
4. If the restaurant is licensed, can you get a license, and is the offer conditional upon this fact?
5. Does the sale of the operation need the landlord's approval? Could this mean a change in the lease, or affect your ability to sell at a later date?

6. Are there any outstanding work orders or liens on the location? (Your lawyer must check.)
7. Has your lawyer checked that all outstanding debts of the restaurant have been or will be paid by the seller? Is that committment in writing and not just verbal?
8. Should you have a non-competitive clause in the sales agreement, to stop the seller opening up a similar restaurant in close proximity?

9

FRANCHISING YOUR DREAM

Why a Franchise?

In addition to buying or building your own restaurant, a third alternative exists—franchising.

There are three distinct advantages to franchising for the first-time restaurateur:

1. The franchisor provides you with a complete package for opening and operating the establishment, which would be very advantageous if you are worried about lack of expertise.
2. There is a lower investment risk because you are selling a proven product in an established market under a recognized name.
3. You would get a quicker return on your investment because of name recognition and corporate advertising; many franchisees realize profits from day one.

However, the successful franchisee still needs sound management skills. The franchise package may set up all the systems and controls, but unless you can carry them out successfully and run your operation efficiently, not only will you have dissatisfied customers, but the franchisor may consider replacing you.

What is a Franchise?

A franchise is a contractual privilege granted by one person or company (the franchisor) to another person or company (the franchisee).

The privilege granted by the franchisor to the franchisee is the right to sell, in a *specified manner,* a particular product or service within a specified territory.

The product or service is usually identified by a trade name, trademark, logo or other commercial symbol over which the franchisor has exclusive control.

The Franchise Fee and What You Get

Once you understand what a franchise is, then you will see that the *franchise fee* is merely a payment to gain the privilege of selling the franchisor's products, following his specific systems, using his trademarks and logos, and within a given area.

In other words, the franchise fee is just like buying a license that can be revoked at any time if you do not obey the terms.

So, apart from certain rights and privileges, what do you get for your franchise fee? This will vary from company to company, but for the first-time operator, you may wish to set the following criteria so as to maximize the potential for success.

1. *Site Selection*—If the franchise company selects the site, the important fact to establish is how they do this (*see* Chapter 6).
2. *Turnkey or Blueprints*—Some companies will provide the site together with a set of blueprints, and tell you to call when you are ready to open. What the first-timer should be looking for is a turnkey operation, which most reputable companies would insist on anyway. But you must still analyze their construction and equipment costs (*see* Chapter 7).
3. *Training*—This should be in two stages: (a) Training for yourself in one of their other locations before your own store is open; (b) In-store training for your staff just prior to and during the opening period.
4. *Operating Manual*—To provide you with ongoing information on how to run your operation smoothly.
5. *Ongoing Backup*—Especially during the critical first few months of operation, or if things are not going too well.
6. *Protected Territory or Area*—After all, you do not want another franchise opening up right opposite you within a few months.

The franchisor/franchisee relationship should be viewed as a partnership, so it is essential to pick a partner that you can work with.

Case Study—Two Brothers and the Donut Shop

Peter and Tony Brown, two brothers, bought a Danny Donut Shop franchise early in the year. They paid the franchisor $12,000. But now, to their dismay, their total commitment is almost $100,000 which they have had to cover with loans, guarantees, and a personal mortgage. Peter and Tony are not happy with their situation.

"We're making money, but . . ." said Tony, one evening after they had closed. "I know," replied Peter, "but not as much as we expected. We should have checked those market estimates that the franchisor gave us."

"We could have spoken to that other Danny Donut Shop franchisee out in the suburbs. He'd have given us a good idea of what to expect."

"Well, there's a new Danny Donut Shop coming into town. Do you want to do a good deed and talk to him?" suggested Peter.

"What do you mean, another franchisee?" asked Tony indignantly. "The city is our territory!"

"The contract we signed says the city is our territory in the sense that we have the right of first refusal on any new franchises. Do you think we can afford to buy another Danny Donut Shop franchise?" asked Peter.

"No way," said Tony shaking his head. "Not after all the money we had to lay out for equipment and fixtures. Sure the franchise purchase price was a good deal, but I thought we could have bought just any equipment and preferably secondhand."

"Our contract specified new equipment. And, as you know, it specified the type of cookers, counters, everything in fact that we needed, along with the supply source."

"Okay," interrupted Tony, "the shop looks nice but they wouldn't even let us modify the layout. If we had smaller tables, we could get more people in. But our franchisor said no."

"It's all in the contract," answered Peter flatly. "Just like I had to say no to that fellow who said he could sell us donut batter cheaper than we buy from the franchisor."

"Why say no?" asked Tony. "That's the only way we can increase our margin, seeing that the franchisor won't let us adjust our retail prices."

"Sorry, Tony. The contract says we buy our batter and all other supplies from the franchisor."

Driving home with Tony, Peter remembered something else concerning their Danny Donut Shop franchise. "I got a call from the franchisor's agent, today. We're late on our six-month royalty payment."

"What do you mean by a royalty payment? We paid the purchase price and we pay a service fee. What is this royalty business?" queried Tony.

"That is in the contract also," explained Peter patiently. "Over a certain volume of sales, we must pay the franchisor a royalty."

"And of course," added Tony, "the franchisor is always sending his agent down to check our operations and to see our books. So he'll always know what our sales are."

"They have to send someone down to make sure that Danny Donut Shop standards are the same everywhere. We've agreed to operate by their rules. It's in the contract," said Peter.

"It's a pity that you know the contract only now," commented Tony bitterly.

"It's both our faults," retorted Peter. "We should have examined the contract more carefully and should have checked out everything about the franchise first."*

The Advantages

Let us look at some of the advantages to buying a franchise.

1. You get operational training.
2. You have the right to use a trade name or trademarks.
3. You are able to sell a proven product and/or service that already has public acceptance.
4. You buy the package so you are able to start full operation sooner.
5. Less start-up capital may be required.
6. Profit-and-loss forecasts may be more accurate.
7. Statistically, you have a better chance of success.
8. There is a defined sales territory, with no other franchisee within a certain radius.
9. You benefit from corporate advertising.

---

*Reprinted from Volume 3 of the "Minding Your Own Business" series published by the Federal Business Development Bank P.O. Box 6021, Station A, Montreal, Quebec H3C 3C3.

10. Depending on the type of franchise, you may be the only source of that particular product.
11. The fixtures, equipment, and premises are often specified or provided by the franchisor.
12. You benefit from recipes and standard controls that have been tested and proven.
13. The franchisor may supply the product or you may benefit from his buying power.
14. The franchisor may be able to arrange financing through his company or a banking service.

The Disadvantages

There are certain things you will have to consider or give up when buying a franchise.

1. You have to pay an up-front franchise fee before you start paying for your location.
2. You are not normally allowed to expand your menu, even if there is a need in your area.
3. The bad reputation that another franchisee may have could affect your business.
4. You have to contribute to corporate advertising whether you want it or not.
5. You may be obliged to buy only from the franchisor.
6. You have to live up to very high standards, or be in jeopardy of losing your franchise.
7. In most cases you have to pay a royalty, from 2 percent to 8 percent of sales.
8. Everyone has to wear the same uniform, including the franchisee.
9. A franchisee often feels as if he is working for a large corporation.
10. You still have to find and train your own staff.
11. You must accept criticism from the franchisor.
12. Depending on the size of the company, backup is not always available.
13. When you buy a franchise, you may not be buying anything but the use of the facilities.
14. Prices may be controlled by head office.

Investigate Before Buying

Just because you are buying a franchise, it does not mean that all the previous points we have discussed in the book can be ignored. And as good as the statistics are for success in operating a franchise, even the best companies have losers. So preparing the business plan and checking the location criteria are still very important.

Before the franchise company grants you a franchise, they will want to interview you and check you out financially and personally to see if you are the type of person they want to operate one of their locations. But, in turn, you should do the same thing. Here are some of the questions you should ask, and then check out:

1. Who are the principals of the company and what are their backgrounds in the foodservice industry?
2. How long has the company been in business, particularly in your area?
3. How quickly has the company grown? Is it a steady planned growth, or a rapid uncontrolled expansion?
4. How many failures has the company had and why?
5. What sort of training and backup does the company provide and what is their staff structure to administer this?
6. What are all the costs you will incur before you open and once you are in operation? Write down what you are told, then check this with your franchise agreement.

Any reputable company would not be insulted by these types of questions. In fact, they should be impressed with your shrewd business approach.

The second step you should take in checking out the franchise company is to talk to other franchisees. Find out if the company does what it says, and what problems the franchisee has had in its dealings with the company. Ask if the sales figures you have been given sound right and if there is an association of franchisees?

Once you have gathered all the information from the first two steps, take it to your lawyer and accountant and ask them to explain everything again, from their understanding of the franchise agreement. If there are things that do not match, then clarify these points before signing the agreement. Some of the questions they should be able to answer from the agreement are:

1. Exactly what do you own or control?
2. Will/when will your ownership or license expire?
3. How long has the company been in existence?
4. What sort of reputation does it have?
5. Are the projected sales figures realistic?
6. Who decides the location?
7. If you are a sub-lessee, how long is it for?
8. Is the equipment owned or leased by the franchise company?
9. What territorial rights do you have?
10. What happens if the franchise company goes under?

Most franchise companies are reputable, especially if they have been in business for some time and have a good track record. However, never take anything at face value; always check. And remember, if it's not in writing, it doesn't mean a thing.

Buyer Beware

Recently, a large Canadian daily newspaper ran a headline: "Listed as a Giant, but franchise firm has few outlets." The story went on to expose a fast-food and restaurant company that was selling franchises and was listed in a nationally circulated directory as having 338 outlets in Canada and over 1,000 outlets in the United States. These figures were given to the directory by the franchise company and published unchecked. The article went on to establish that, although the company was indeed selling franchises, everything from submarine take-outs to licensed steakhouses, it had very few, if any, locations actually open and operating.

It is interesting to note that the same newspaper had given the franchise company a favorable write-up only nine months before, as had many other newspapers and trade magazines.

Franchising and the Law

The laws covering franchising vary from state to state and must be fully understood before any agreement is signed.

Naturally, your lawyer can complete the necessary investigative work for you, but if you wish to know more about franchising or a particular company, without incurring legal fees, then there is another way.

The International Franchise Association, (I. F. A.) located in Washington, D.C. is a self-regulating trade association of franchise companies, that oversee their own industry. Not only can you gain valuable information about the franchising laws in your state, but also if a particular company is a member of the I. F. A. in good standing and other background information about the company.

10

HOW TO PROTECT YOUR INVESTMENT

Although the legal end of any business is normally of the least interest to most business entrepreneurs and first-time owners, it should be high on your list of priorities.

Because of lack of interest and knowledge, the type of ownership and safeguards is normally only considered out of necessity, and not as part of the business plan.

For the small business owner, there are several ways to set up your company, and each way has its advantages and disadvantages. Discussion with your lawyer and accountant will help you decide which way is best for you.

It should be qualified that what may be advantageous today may be a disadvantage tomorrow, simply because the laws covering business ownership (normally taxes) are constantly changing with almost every budget or mini-budget.

Before you go to your lawyer for the expert advice you will need to set up your restaurant business structure, you might consider reading all about the different kinds of business organizations available. An excellent book, for just that kind of overview is *The Financial Handbook,* edited by Mr. Jules I. Bogen, Ph.D.; published by The Ronald Press Company of New York, copyright 1968. This book will give you much to think about, and most of the information is current due to recent updates.

Types of Business Structure

The three most common ways of structuring your business are:

1. Proprietorship   3. Corporation
2. Partnership

The following outline deals with some of the generalities you may wish to consider, but your lawyer or accountant should be consulted before a final decision is made.

Proprietorship

A proprietorship is an unincorporated company, owned by one person. It is the easiest and cheapest way of starting your business.

You simply have to *register* your business, under the name you wish to operate under, with the appropriate state or local authority, pay a small fee, and away you go. As a sole proprietor, you personally are entitled to all the profits from your business. These profits become your personal income. At the year-end you would simply file your own income-tax return, entering the profits from your business as your self-employed income, and pay the necessary taxes that apply, at whatever rate is applicable.

On the other side of the coin, the proprietor is personally responsible for any debts the business may incur, especially if things aren't going too well. If your business fails, then your creditors can come after you, and anything that you own (house, car, etc.).

Partnership

A partnership is a business set up by two or more people with a common goal—to make a profit. The partnership has to be *registered* with the appropriate state or local authority and, again, is an inexpensive set-up, except for the fact that a partnership agreement should be drawn up by a lawyer. This agreement should specify the following points:

1. Contribution of each partner (time, money, etc.)
2. Duties of each partner
3. How profits or losses are divided
4. Signing officers of the partnership
5. Voting arrangement in making decisions
6. Method in which new partners can leave the firm
7. What happens in the event of the death of a partner

Different Types of Partners
There are four different types of partners:

1. *Active*—One who works in the business and may have contributed cash.
2. *Silent*—One who has normally contributed cash and may lend some expertise to the business, normally behind the scenes.
3. *Ostensible*—One who has no financial interest in the partnership, but lends his name and credit to the business.
4. *Limited*—One who assumes no liability to the partnership beyond his initial financial contribution.

A general partnership is an association of two or more partners, both with unlimited liability for the debts of the business. Most partnership agreements must be in writing to meet the requirements of the statute of frauds in most states. Partners who share the unlimited liability also share in any profits. This kind of business structure or organization is in a common law form, and many states have adopted statutes governing the relationship of partners to one another and to those with whom the partnership has dealings. The Uniform Partnership Act has been adopted by most states and the District of Columbia.

This form of organization is very complicated, and you should query your lawyer completely about it before proceeding.

The partnership form of organization is superior to the proprietorship because it permits several persons to combine their resources and abilities to make a business, and it is easier to form than a corporation.

Lastly, the partnership is at somewhat of a disadvantage. With the unlimited liability of the partners, the relative instability of the form, and the difficulty in attracting outside capital, it is a form that exists only among small- and medium-sized businesses.

Incorporation
Incorporating your own company is the most expensive form of business ownership, but often considered the best. An incorporated company is a separate legal entity or, in other words, the company is a person. You as the incorporator are not responsible for the debts of the company, but as a shareholder are entitled to

a share of the profits, according to the percentage of shares you own.

Incorporating the company is usually done by a lawyer, and may cost you between $800 to $1,000, depending on the complexity of the share structure. However, many people now find it possible to incorporate their own company themselves, with the help of any of the "how-to" books now on the market. Check your local library for these books, and follow the guides exactly. Although it may take some of your time, it will cost you a lot less. This route is only advisable if the company you are incorporating has only a simple share structure, involving one or two shareholders, i.e., you and your spouse.

The advantages of incorporating are far greater than the other two forms of business ownership.

1. Although you are the incorporator and a shareholder, you will also be an employee of the company, drawing a salary, as can your spouse, if he or she is working in the business.
2. Your liability is limited to the amount of money you spent in purchasing your shares, which can be minimal. If the company fails, it is the company that owes the money, not you.

   The only exception would be if you signed any personal guarantees with suppliers, banks, landlords, etc. You are then responsible to those individuals. Money lenders will always want your personal guarantee.
3. It becomes very easy for other people to buy into the company, especially employees, with whom you might want to share the profits.
4. The company doesn't die with the owner; it is a separate entity and, as such, has immortality.
5. To sell the business, the owner would simply have to sell his shares, as long as this transaction conforms to the shareholders agreement and by-laws of the company.
6. There can be certain tax advantages in incorporating, although this is questionable at the present time. However, there is more opportunity to write off certain expenses as company costs. This should be done only on a legitimate basis; if too much is written off, it may affect your ability to sell your company in the future as the profit you are showing is very small.

7. An incorporated company seems to get better treatment from suppliers and other creditors as far as terms are concerned although I've never understood why.

The disadvantages of incorporating are as follows:
1. Most expensive and involved form of business set-up.
2. More ongoing costs with record keeping, accounting, and legal requirements.
3. Corporations are more closely regulated by government.

The Legal Requirements

Municipal
When buying, building, or franchising a restaurant in any location within a municipality you must check that the location you have chosen is correct within municipal guidelines and by-laws. This is usually done during the planning stages by your lawyer. He can check into the correct municipal regulations and by-laws concerning zoning, parking regulations, by-law exemptions, land uses, planning guidelines, etc.

Occupancy Permits
Often, in municipalities, you must first purchase an occupancy permit from the municipality. This usually entails providing city hall with copies of your lease, a letter from you stating your prospective use of the location, a small fee plus a set dollar figure based on the cost of the building, renovation, etc., and about a 10-day wait while your application is authorized and issued. If your location is okay, this is generally an easy process.

Building Permits
This application is generally filed much later than the preceding one. At the time of application, you must provide city hall with *sealed* copies of the plans completed by both your designer (for layouts, etc.) and *sealed* copies of plans completed by mechanical engineers (showing all services, utilities, etc.). As well, the cost of building permits can be high. Not only is there a fee, but a sliding scale of dollars based on the total cost of building the operation. It is at this point that the municipality will check all plans for

their conformance to the building code with respect to materials and finishes, fire regulations, zoning, plumbing, and electrical wiring. The municipality must be notified by the local department of health that it meets their requirements also.

This can be a lengthy process, perhaps lasting a month. But until a building permit is issued, no work can begin on the restaurant. As well, throughout the building construction, city inspectors will visit the job site to ensure that your contractors are following the plans exactly. Upon completion of the construction, city inspectors will do a final inspection and issue letters to you allowing you to commence business.

Department of Health

This is a municipal body concerned with public health in the community. A set of plans must also be tendered to them for approval. They are most concerned with food storage, handling, cooking, equipment, and with sanitation (garbage) handling areas, as well as public washrooms and bar areas. They also have a required list of regulations and guidelines that you must meet during normal operations. They will notify the municipality of your compliance to their codes, do a final inspection to see that you have followed your own plans, and issue a letter allowing you to open.

Fire Departments

They are also concerned with building code regulations. Your design okayed by the city will have to conform with that code, and the local fire department will make inspections to see that it does. They are most concerned with the fire ratings of building materials, exits, entrances, sprinklers and fire alarms, and structural codes. As well, they will inspect periodically to ensure that you are not overcrowding the premises.

Utilities

The restaurateur usually deals with the utility companies—electricity, gas, telephone—and installation of their metering devices. Plans are often necessary for electric companies and gas companies to approve before installation, along with estimated fees based on the extent of service, etc. Deposits based on estimated usage are often required for these utility companies. And often, these utility companies will be required to issue a letter of approval of inspection to your state liquor board before you can go and get your liquor licence.

State and Federal Concerns

When you have decided to form your business into one of the several different business organizations, your lawyer and accountant will then be able to advise you on what else you now need to know. Because the requirements vary so widely from state to state, you might be responsible for a great many different items to satisfy your legal requirements. Make sure you pay strict attention to the experts you've hired; their advice should be both listened to . . . and followed to the letter.

Insurance

The first important step towards fulfilling your insurance needs is to choose the right agent. Determining what previous dealings and experience the agent has had in the restaurant industry will tell you whether this person can be helpful to you, or will just be learning on your time. It is important to tell the agent accurately all the costs and requirements involved with your operation. Your lease may require certain coverages that you are not aware of, so the agent should be given a copy of your lease so as to make sure you meet all the specifications as listed.

It is also important that your agent visit your premises, so he or she can fully understand your requirements. This visit may also prompt suggestions from your agent that may not have surfaced if the transactions had been completed by phone.

Although it is impossible to specify exactly the kind of insurance that your operation will require, the following areas should be considered and discussed with your agent.

Fire

Because of the very nature of the restaurant industry, fire is a constant cause for concern. There are two important areas to consider. The first is that you insure your restaurant and its contents at replacement cost, simply because that is what it will cost you. The second area of concern is to determine the total loss a fire could cause, especially if you are attached to other buildings or you are located within a shopping mall.

General Liability

This can cover several areas, but as an example, consider this situation. A customer gets drunk in your restaurant, and immediately after leaving is involved in a serious car accident in which someone else is fatally injured. As a consequence, you could be sued, because you were responsible for allowing that customer to get drunk on your premises.

Inventory Coverage

Another area to consider is covering your inventory against loss through such things as power failures, which could cause all your frozen and refrigerated products to spoil. However, it is important to calculate how much the deduction would be for this kind of coverage, and how much your total loss may be at any one time. When you have assessed this, you may find that this insurance is unjustified.

Business Interruption

This type of insurance is often overlooked. If your restaurant is closed because of fire damage, your insurance would cover all replacement costs. But what about the loss of income to you as the owner? If you have a good staff, and you don't want to lose them, you may feel it is necessary to continue paying them during this period of closure. Your business interruption coverage will at least provide income to meet this and other obligations you may have to fulfill, such as rent, etc.

Crime Insurance

This covers you against such things as hold-up and theft. You may also wish to consider bonding key personnel who control or have access to cash or inventory, such as liquor.

Automobile Insurance

This would be necessary in two situations:

1. If your vehicle is an asset of the company, or
2. If you or a member of staff is involved in an accident in a privately owned car, but while they or you were on company business. The injured party may consider it more advantageous to sue your company than the car's owner.

Key Person or Life Insurance

Key person insurance is often taken out when a partnership is involved. The non-active partner will insure the life of the active partner, and this would supply cash to either hire a manager in the interim, so that another active partner can be found, or to buy out the shares of the deceased partner so that the business can be easily sold. Life insurance should also be considered by the owner/operator, as the business may quickly deteriorate after his or her death. Cash could be drained from the business and personal savings, if the remaining spouse is left with a business he or she is unable to operate.

Benefit Insurance

This type of coverage is now available to even the smallest of companies. You can provide group, dental, and life insurance as a staff benefit, or as a benefit for the owner/operator. Your regular insurance agent may not actually deal in this specific area, but should be able to make recommendations.

Timing is a very important aspect of the total insurance package. Your premises should be insured either with the commencement of your lease or from the time you take possession, whichever is sooner. The landlord may allow you possession before the lease-date commencement, but if any accidents or damages occur, he may hold you or your company responsible. Insurance is certainly not an area in which to try to save pennies!

11

HIRED GUNS—THE EXPERTS YOU WILL NEED

Qualifying the Experts

If you are a prospective restaurateur and need advice about the procedures necessary to open a foodservice operation, your best bet is to deal only with experts. Checking out or qualifying the experts you are planning to retain is the first step you must take. They should have experience in, and knowledge of, the restaurant business in order to give you the advice you are seeking and, most likely, paying for.

Suppose you are going to buy a franchise and have decided to take the franchise agreement to your family lawyer. In the past you have received good service from this lawyer and you feel comfortable with him. But if you stop to recall your legal transactions with this lawyer, you will begin to realize that they probably involved the sale or purchase of a house, the drawing up of a will, or a minor legal offence such as a traffic violation. Has your lawyer ever dealt with a franchise agreement? This is a fact you must ascertain in order to ensure that your best interests are served. Forget that you like this man or that you think he might do the job for less money. In the long run, his lack of experience in the restaurant field might cost you more than you can afford.

A visit to your family doctor is a good analogy of this situation. If the problem is minor, he or she will prescribe the necessary cure, and all is well. But if your ailment is more complex, your family doctor will suggest that you see a specialist who deals only in that particular area of medicine. Lawyers, and many other experts, are no different from doctors, in that they often specialize in certain areas of their given field. It is up to you to decide if this particular person can give you the help you need, or if you should retain the help of a specialist.

The Initial Interview

The first meeting you have with any potential expert should be treated as an interview. Remember, you are the customer, the person who is going to pay the bill, so don't be intimidated or afraid to ask all the relevant questions regarding this person's past experience. Ask for references or to see other work of a similar nature that this person or company has completed. If they are any good, they will be only too happy to boast of their accomplishments. This is also the time to establish the expert's fee structure: the amount and the various alternatives, hourly rate, daily rate, project rate, or cost plus percentage. Make sure you fully understand not only how much the work is going to cost, but when you are expected to pay—up-front, on completion, or payments over the period of work. All of these questions will not only help you establish your total budget, but will also let the person you are dealing with know that you are a business-minded individual and are not going to accept any unnecessary or exorbitant fees or costs.

Dealing with Experts

Dealing with experts, either at the initial or subsequent meeting, can be an expensive proposition, especially if you are paying for their services by the hour. So the key thing to remember is to be well prepared before you have your meeting. The following points should help in this preparation.

1. First, you should only deal with experts who have the knowledge to help you, not just those that you like or feel comfortable with.
2. Prepare all the questions that you can think of in advance and write them down. This will not only save you time, but if the expert is charging by the hour, it can also save you money.
3. Take notes at the meeting. You may forget a lot of the conversation afterwards.

4. If there is something you don't understand, say so, and ask the person you are dealing with to explain the point again.
5. Always ask for quotes or estimates in writing, specifying costs, fees, timing, etc. If, for some reason, this is not possible, then confirm the points of the discussion in writing, following the meeting.
6. Be open-minded and hear what you are told, not just what you want to hear.
7. Never get angry if you don't get what you want (especially if you are dealing with a bank manager). Try to learn from the experience.
8. Ask the experts you are dealing with if they can recommend other experts that you might need. For example, your lawyer may be able to recommend a good accountant.
9. Always try to see more than one expert in each field. This not only allows you to compare cost, but also style, knowledge, and compatibility.
10. Finally, never be afraid to dangle a carrot in front of an expensive expert. Suggest that someday you may be a very good client, indeed, and one who remembers favors granted in the early days.

Experts Who Charge

The first category of experts we are going to discuss are those who will charge you a fee for their services, regardless of the outcome of your dealings with them.

Lawyers
They can be very helpful in several areas. They will, of course, handle all legal contracts and negotiations, advise you on all the legal requirements in starting your business, and act on your behalf in obtaining various permits and licenses. They can also be very helpful in finding partners or investors from within their own client list.

Accountants
They can also be a good source for funding or obtaining partners. Their main help will be in the preparation of your financial projections and they will even accompany you when you are applying to

your lender. From the figures you supply, they may be able to point out problem areas they see. Accountants will also be of help on an ongoing basis with the preparation of yearly statements and returns.

Market Analysts
They will, from the information you supply regarding concept and location, determine if there is a market for your type of restaurant.

Consultants
These experts can be a great help by advising the prospective restaurateur on all aspects of the business, from analyzing the initial concept feasibility to staffing, opening the location, and everything in-between.

Designers/Architects
They are the people that formulate the design that will complement your restaurant concept. They will also coordinate all necessary codes and regulations, so that your operation will open without problems from the municipal regulatory bodies.

Mechanical Engineers
Working normally with the designer, they are the people who will plan your plumbing, electrical, air conditioning, heating, and exhausting needs.

Experts Who Sell

The experts listed in this category do not charge for the advice that they give, but it must be remembered that, because their primary job is to sell the products of the company they represent, their advice will be biased. It is up to you to evaluate each company's products, and make the decision that best suits you. When dealing with a company that is selling a particular piece of equipment, always ask where you can see that equipment in use. This gives you the opportunity to discuss its performance with a similar operator.

Kitchen Equipment Companies
They will be able to provide all the equipment you require for the preparation, cooking, and service areas. Many companies also provide a complete design service for your kitchen and service areas, but

normally this service is free only if you purchase the equipment from them. If, after they have completed the design work, you decide to buy your equipment elsewhere, they will then invoice you for the designs they have provided.

Many companies also deal in used equipment. But, although the initial costs may be lower, you will have to consider what you are giving up by way of warranties. The net result could be little, if any savings.

Furniture Companies

They can be very helpful in locating the type of furnishings that will complement your concept. The range in prices can sometimes be very wide, so it is advisable to shop around. It is important to realize that furnishings must be of industrial rather than household quality, so they will be able to stand up to heavy usage in the restaurant.

Sound System Companies

Sound system companies are a fast-growing industry. It is essential to use a company that sells equipment that will stand up to from twelve to sixteen hours of use each day. It is also important to use a company that has the expertise to install the equipment, so the sound system is well-balanced throughout your operation.

Bar System Companies

They will provide you with various types of control systems, greatly varying in price and quality. The system best for you will depend on the kind of volumes that you anticipate as well as the person who will be serving the liquor. Again, discussions with other users in similar operations will give you a better idea of the system best for you.

Cash Control System Companies

They are probably as numerous as the different types of restaurants in existence. As with the bar system, it is important to anticipate the kind of volumes you expect, the type of information you require, and the person who will be handling the cash. A look at similar operations will give you a better idea. These companies should also provide full training in the use of the system as part of the price.

Security System Companies
They may be required, depending on the location of your operation. Again, there are many systems available, but your insurance agent may be able to help you in this regard.

Uniform Companies
These companies have many different styles and designs readily available. They will also design uniforms for your specific operation, but as with the kitchen equipment companies, these designs are offered free of charge, as long as you purchase the uniforms from them. It is also important, when selecting a custom design, to ascertain the reorder period and minimum quantities, especially if you do not have a particularly large operation.

Printing Companies
Printing companies will also provide facilities to complete artwork suggestions, as long as they get the final order. During busy times of the year, you may have to wait from four to six weeks for delivery, so don't leave this item to the last minute. As well as the menus, they can also provide other printed items such as matches, napkins, guest checks, and various bar accessories.

Advertising and Promotional Companies
These companies can also provide promotional materials such as matches, key rings, pens—in fact just about anything that you want your name on in an effort to promote your operation. It is important not to get too carried away in this area and blow your annual advertising budget in the first month.

The Free Experts

Not only are free experts often the best, they are probably the most overlooked. The first two in this section, the manager and the chef, can be the most valuable of all the experts, if you have to hire people to fill these positions.

Manager
If hired prior to opening, the manager can save the new restaurateur a considerable amount of time and money, as his or her previous experience can offset a lot of costly mistakes. The manager can pro-

vide expertise on systems, controls, staffing, and most of the areas previously covered.

Hiring a manager can also help you to obtain financing. Many lending institutions are hesitant to loan funds to an inexperienced restaurateur; but if they know you have, or are going to hire an experienced manager, it can make the difference.

Chef

A chef can be another valuable asset to the first-timer, especially if your menu is complex or you have absolutely no idea about what is required. If you feel that hiring a manager and a chef would be of help to you, prior to opening you may wish to consider their previous experience in opening restaurant operations. There is a great deal of difference between opening a restaurant and running an existing one.

Bank Managers

They have had experience in opening new businesses, and they may be able to provide contacts. It is often the case that they will not offer their help unless it is requested, but then they are only too happy to provide any assistance they can.

The bank manager often knows of restaurants for sale in the area or quality prospective sellers or franchisors, can check credit references of contractors and suppliers, advise you on your business plan and many other areas—all at no cost to you.

Insurance Agents

They are constantly moving around the business community and may be able to provide valuable information. Your agent could also be a source of funding, through clients he knows are looking for good investments.

Real Estate Agents

Real estate agents are another source of information. They often know of properties that will be, or might be coming onto the market. It must be remembered that the agent only makes money when the property is sold, so the information you receive could be biased.

Franchisees
They can provide a lot of inside information about the franchise company you may be considering. Their advice should be unbiased, but it is advisable to talk to more than one, in order to get a broad picture.

Family and Friends
These people are often overlooked as a source of expertise. Sometimes we don't know exactly what kind of business a relative or friend is in. It never hurts to ask what everyone does for a living within your immediate circle.

Partners
They may seem an obvious source of expertise, but if there are ten or more investors involved, it can sometimes be overlooked. Just by checking the present and past business experiences of each partner, you may turn up a free expert with a vested interest in making the business a success.

Suppliers
They are not normally contacted until the restaurant is close to operation, but talking to local sales staff, as a prospective customer, can provide a great deal of inside information about a restaurant that is up for sale, or that has recently closed.

The Better Business Bureau
The Better Business Bureau can be used to obtain information regarding franchise companies, contractors, suppliers, and other companies you may be considering. This service is available to members and nonmembers alike, and can be accessed by a simple phone call.

Reference Sources
Reference sources such as libraries, U.S. government statistics, trade and local associations, business and trade publications, banks, savings and loans, and the many government—both state and federal—agencies, all provide booklets and reference material that can be of great use to the prospective restaurateur. By utilizing the services of the business section of your local library, sources of material, names and addresses of publications and agencies can be easily obtained.

Conclusion

In summarizing your dealings with any expert, there are three points that apply at all times.

1. Is the expert qualified or experienced enough to provide the services that you require?
2. Have you shopped around to compare the price and style of various experts?
3. Is the expert whom you are dealing with biased in any way? Does the expert stand to profit from the advice he or she gives?

12

SYSTEMS AND CONTROLS

Control really means controlling people rather than things. That is, control is the process by which managers attempt to direct, regulate, and restrain the actions of people, in order to achieve desired goals.

Now those people are not only staff, but include delivery men, servicemen, and so forth. They all use your new restaurant to earn a living, directly or indirectly. Any of the difficulties that could arise are the result of human action, or lack of it, and if your restaurant is to succeed according to plan, it is the actions of people that must be controlled.

In order to ensure that your restaurant succeeds, you must first understand that the responsibility for control rests with you, and you alone. A number of factors, including the nature and scope of your restaurant, will dictate the extent to which you delegate that responsibility. But remember, the ultimate responsibility is yours.

Basically, there are five tactics to effectively control your new restaurant, and you should be aware of them before you open. They are as follows:

1. Standards
2. Systems
3. Management Style
4. Staff Training
5. Staff Monitoring

Standards

Simply put, standards are measures set by you in order to make a judgment, or a decision. This decision will enable you to compare your actual restaurant operations with what you had planned and expected.

To enable you to understand these standards, remember that there are three you must plan beforehand: (1) quality, (2) quantity, (3) actual versus potential standards.

Quality

The term "quality standards" refers to the degree of excellence of raw or finished materials and a subtle spin-off, staff work or productivity levels. You must establish these quality standards for many areas of your new restaurant. For instance, when you are buying beef, you must be aware of the different grades of each item you purchase. And when that steak or prime rib is consumed by your customers you must be aware that their satisfaction is based on that quality. The same holds true for all of your menu items, since your customers rate that quality against the selling price, the "perceived value" of their meal. To ensure that the perceived value is high, you must insist on quality standards, even in your staff. A high degree of skill or quality is often required by members of your staff, like managers and chefs, to ensure your restaurant's success.

Quantity

Quantity standards refer to measures of size and weight. You must establish such quantity standards as portion sizes for food and beverage items, and work output for employees.

In setting up your quantity standards, you must clearly establish the portion size for all your menu items, both food and beverage, from predetermining that there will be eight chicken wings in each and every order to 1 oz. of vodka in every screwdriver. This will require you to compose a recipe file, listing a complete breakdown of each method of preparation. The recipe file system must, of course, be developed early, as a spin-off of your menu creation. It must list every menu item and the recipe and procedure for producing it. As well, if the items are produced in a master batch, for portioning, it must include a cost per ingredient.

Assemble the complete costings, not forgetting to add in any garnish or condiment listings and costs. It also helps to list any utensils needed and the plating necessary to service the item. Your food cost is generated per each individual menu item for use in determining your potential food cost. And by indicating on each menu file card the date of the last cost update, you can see any costing changes by the next update. It is a handy tool to use for the study of food cost changes, and the variance between your potential and actual food cost (*see* Sample #13).

Your staff must also be considered. It is useful to know just how many people are necessary to staff the restaurant, and just what volume of products they can produce.

Actual versus Potential

Actual, versus potential standards are useful in measuring the effectiveness of your new operation. You must first realize that these standards are to be used to measure other costs. For instance, consider a bottle of vodka. If it contains 40 ozs. and costs $12, each ounce then costs 30¢; that is the standard cost of one ounce of vodka that may be used alone in a drink, or as part of a cocktail. But that is only the potential cost. It doesn't allow for spillage, evaporation, or theft, all of which are likely to occur. In the day-to-day operations, many ounces of vodka might be wasted or misused. Those ounces represent lost sales revenue.

When you establish the sales units you did sell, divided by the number you purchased, that will give you your actual usage. And measuring the actual against the potential will show you just how many units were lost—another way to control your restaurant.

Using these actual versus potential standards will determine your profitability, and is a necessary part of comparing what you *are doing* with what you *should be doing*.

Systems

The methods you develop to prepare a food or beverage product or perform a job are systems. These systems are your correct procedures for performing these day-to-day tasks.

You must set up these systems for every stage of production and service of food and beverage items, as well as for your sales/cash controls.

SAMPLE #13 **Recipe File**				
NAME: Ranch House Chili			*FILE #* 37	
YIELD: 32 Portions			*PORTION SIZE:* 1 × 8 oz. Bowl	
INGREDIENTS	*WEIGHTS*	*MEASURES*	*METHOD*	*COSTING*
Bacon, diced, small	5 oz.	8 strips	1. Cook bacon 2. Remove bacon. Save drippings.	.75
Stewing Beef, lean, cut in 1/2 inch cubes. Pork Shoulder, boneless, lean, cut in 1/2 inch cubes.	4 lbs. 4 lbs.	—	3. Brown meats in drippings.	8.12 7.01
Onion, dry, sliced	—	1/2 cup	4. Combine meats with	.21
Garlic, dry, minced	—	1 tsp.	all ingredients.	.09
Oregano, dry	—	1 tbsp.	Bring to boil.	.10
Salt, table	—	4 tsp.		.12
Cumin, ground	—	2 tsp.	Simmer under lid	.19
Coriander, ground	—	2 tsp.	for 1 1/2 hours or	.22
Chiles; green, diced	27 oz.	2 cans	until meat is	12.00
Beef broth	—	3 cups	tender.	1.02
Cooking burgundy	—	3 cups		5.17
Chile Salsa, green	28 oz.	2 cans	5. Recipe complete.	7.00
Tomato sauce	2 lbs.	1 qt.		3.77
Celery, sliced	17 oz.	1 qt.		1.42

GARNISH or CONDIMENT	3 oz. shredded Jack cheese @ .09 per oz.	MASTER BATCH RECIPE COST	47.19
		÷ 32 PORTIONS = PORTION COST	1.47
UTENSILS	Round Soup Spoon	+ CONDIMENT OR GARNISH COST	.27
		TOTAL PORTION COST	1.74
PLATING	White soup bowl holding 8 oz. portion, with salad plate as an underliner.	DATE OF LAST COSTING October 13, 19—	

First systemize your ordering and buying procedures to ensure that your products come to you in the needed quantities and quality. Then consider your receiving procedures: are you getting the right products and at the right price? And are you storing products to guard against theft, waste, and spoilage?

You must then make sure those products are issued properly, rotated uniformly, and put into production on time. Moreover, records of these product-issues must be maintained in order to calculate the actual cost-per-item-produced. This you compare to the potential cost-per-item-produced as estimated in your recipe file. Again, this is another method for increasing profitability.

All of your production procedures must be systemized to ensure that any given menu item is produced the same way every time, in the same quality and quantity, to ensure customer satisfaction and a continuity of standards.

When your systems are combined with the previous standards, it becomes possible to measure each aspect of your restaurant business.

The day-to-day operating realities should be compared to your combined standards and systems. Any variances must be rated, and changes made to bring actual standards and systems more in line with the potential ones you pre-planned. When actual standards and systems compare favorably to the potential, it means effective controls exist.

Obviously, you can't be everywhere at once to observe your staff's actions. The larger your restaurant, the more likely it is that you'll have to rely on a variety of records and reports. Some of the ones you should consider are listed below.

Requisition Forms

These forms indicate the quantity of products requisitioned from storage by the kitchen and bar staff. They will be measured against your sales analysis form to see if what was requisitioned and then produced was sold. If not, where did these items go (*see* Sample #14).

Production Forms

These forms are meant for daily use by the kitchen staff to enable them to produce enough food items for each day's business volume. Generally drawn up by your chef, it will ensure both

SAMPLE #14		
Requisition Form		

To:	Main Kitchen	*Date:* Aug. 31, 19—

Quantity	Description
6	#10 Cans—Whole Tomatoes
5	10 lb. bags—Frozen hamburger
20 lbs.	Whole grain rice
18	Heads of Cabbage
6 lbs.	Bread Crumbs
30	Onions—Medium
24	Eggs—Large
Usage:	(1) Master Batch of Cabbage Rolls, yielding 240 portions
Charge To:	Food Cost
Signature:	—Chef

accountability of product and that you won't overproduce with resulting waste (*see* Sample #15).

Daily Cash Report
This report (*see* Sample #16) should break down your daily sales into categories. You'll want to know not only that each server or cashier remitted the correct amounts, but also the breakdown of cash, credit-card vouchers, and house accounts for your banking and accounting purposes. This report is then compiled into weekly, then monthly totals for your sales control analysis.

Sample #16 outlines the various things you will need to know in order to balance your daily cash.

1. Register Sales of $2,341.65 represent the sales totals from all cash register machines.
2. Opening Float is the amount of money you have on hand every day to run your restaurant. You'll need it for cash purchases, floats for your cash registers, etc. It's a constant amount that will be on hand, every day you're open.
3. Cash Purchases can be many things, as shown. You list the item first (food costs, beverage costs, and other operating expenses), then post each item to the department where it will eventually be totaled.
4. Subtotal #1 is, of course, the float minus your cash purchases for the day.
5. Sales by Server is a list of the names of each server working on that particular day, and the amount of sales each server had accumulated. Every staff member who is responsible for taking cash should be on this list, including waiters/ waitresses, cashiers, bar staff, etc.
6. Subtotal #2 is the total of all these points of sales and should be the same total as Register Sales.
7. Over/Short is the difference between Subtotal #2 and Register Sales. Any substantial variance between these two totals, whether Over or Short, is a cause for concern, and shows that your cash-control system is breaking down.
8. Total Cash On Hand is attained by the addition of Subtotals #1 and #2, allowing for any cash Overs or Shorts.
9. Bank Deposit is the total of your Cash On Hand less your $500 Opening Float. The only variance to this total happens

SAMPLE #15						
Daily Production Form				*DATE:*	October 1, 19—	
ITEM	*FORMAT*	*HOLDING STATE*	*ON HAND*	*USAGE*	*PREPARATION TASK*	*INI-TIAL*
Chicken Wings	50 lb. Box	frozen	21 lbs.	100 lbs. daily	Thaw (2) boxes tonight	
Lasagna	8 portions per tray	frozen	12 portions	36 portions	Thaw (2) trays in cooler overnight	
B.B.Q. Sauce	4 × 128 oz.	Unspiced in storage	1 × 128 oz. spiced	4 × 128 oz. weekly		
Pre-Cooked Apple Pie	6 per case	frozen	2	4 daily	Thaw (1) case in cooler	
Iceberg Lettuce	24 per case	Fresh uncleaned	5 heads	15 heads	Wash, clean, trim (1) case & store in cooler overnight in sealed bags.	
Strip Loins (A1–A2)—(10–12 lbs. avg.)	(1) piece yields 14 portions	frozen	9 portions	15 portions	Thaw (1) strip loin in cooler overnight in pan to catch all water & blood. See recipe #37 for prep.	
Shrimp (P&D) 41/50 count	3 lb. bags yield 10 portions	frozen	7 portions	11 portions	Thaw (1) bag overnight in cooler See recipe #21 for prep.	

SAMPLE #16					
DATE:	Oct. 1, 19—	*MGR:*	J. Rudnick	*REG. SALES*	2,341.65

DAILY CASH REPORT					
Opening Float	500.00	CASH PURCHASES			
Less Cash Purchases	−59.75	ITEM	POST	COST	
Subtotal #1	440.25	Ketchup	Food Cost	11.25	
SALES BY SERVER		Lettuce	Food Cost	27.00	
Janice (Day Cashier)	376.55	Stamps	Office	6.50	
Nancy	310.20	Rug Cleaning	Service	15.00	
Betty	291.85				
Ruth (Night Cashier)	263.95				
Sue	141.65				
Darlene	315.75				
Debbie	332.80	TOTAL		59.75	
Angie	310.80	Remarks: _____			
Subtotal #2	2,343.55				
Over/Short +	(1.90)				
Add—Subtotal #1	440.25				
TOTAL CASH ON HAND	2,783.80				
LESS OPENING FLOAT	500.00				
BANK DEPOSIT	2,283.80				

if you accept charge-card vouchers which you have to redeem from the card company or from another bank. If this is the case, then it is advisable to keep a separate record of these transactions.

Sales Analysis Report
This report is generated from your cash register. It should list the sales by each server of every menu item sold, by food and beverage groupings. It is used to analyze how productive each server was that day, which need more training or a lesser work load in order to cope, and to analyze which menu items sell well and which don't. If a normally good seller has slackened off, why? Are your standards and systems not being followed, and has that put your customers off? As well, comparing this actual listing of sold menu items to your requisition and production forms will tell you if you're losing products before they get to your customers.

Inventory Report
This report usually lists every item you buy for eventual production into menu items. Although lengthy, it is a very necessary part of your operation, and is used many ways. If you take a complete inventory on a Sunday, you can measure your "on-hand" levels against your weekly volumes and order, on Monday, up to those levels. A four-week inventory report, with the added purchased items less your on-hand items, will give you your monthly-usage report. This usage report, when extended by unit-dollar values for food and beverage items, can be measured against your accumulated daily-sales reports. This will then give you potential food and beverage costs, and will show you when your standards and systems are not being followed. These are important guidelines for your success. Sample #17 is used as follows:

1. The Item column is used for listing all the food and beverage items that you have in stock. It is advisable to break these down into categories such as meats, produce, dairy products, beverages, dried goods, etc., and subtotal each category for ease of calculating your total inventory.
2. The Unit column should depict the way in which each item will be counted and priced, i.e., lbs., cans, packets, cases, bottles, etc.

SAMPLE #17									
DATE: Oct. 1, 19___ *MGR:* J. Smith		**INVENTORY REPORT**							
ITEM	*UNIT*	*Opening*	*Purchase*	*Total*	*Closing*	*Used*	*UNIT PRICE*	*COST*	*RE-ORDER*
MEATS:									
Chicken Wings	50-lb. box	3½	3	6½	2½	4	45.00	180.00	2
Sliced Bacon	10-lb. box	2	5	7	4	3	19.60	58.80	0
							Subtotal	238.80	
FROZEN VEGETABLE:									
French Fries	30-lb. box	5	20	25	4	21	12.75	267.75	25
Onion Rings	10-lb. box	2	1	3	1	2	8.80	17.60	2
							Subtotal	285.35	
BAR LIQUOR:									
Canadian Club	each	11	–	11	3	8	14.65	117.20	10
J&B Scotch	each	1	6	7	4	3	16.65	49.95	0
Beefeater Gin	each	3	–	3	1	2	15.25	30.50	3
							Subtotal	197.65	
						TOTAL COST:		721.80	

3. The Opening column is, in fact, your closing-inventory figure from the last inventory you completed. For the very first inventory report taken for your operation, there should be no opening figures.
4. The Purchases column would include all the purchases for the period since your last inventory report.
5. The Total column figure is arrived at by adding the Opening and Purchase columns together.
6. The Closing column would be the amount of inventory physically on hand, taken at the end of the period.
7. The Used column is the sum of the Total column, less the Closing column, and tells you what has actually been used in your operation during the period.

8. Unit Price is the most recent price of each item, reduced to the unit by which it is counted, as depicted in the Unit column.

9. Cost is arrived at by multiplying the Unit Price by the number of units used (from the Used column). The sum of this column, Total Cost, will give you the total amount of food and beverages used in a given period.

10. The Re-Order column is a handy device for instantly recognizing what is, or should be, needed for the next period of operation. You now know what has been used and what you have left, so it is quite easy to calculate what you should reorder.

Note:

The completion of a physical inventory report is quite time consuming; but it is the only way to measure how well you and your staff are controlling the operations' cost of sales. For the new owner, a weekly report should be completed until such a time as you think everything is running as it should be. Then you can drop down to a monthly report. However, if at any time the food costs start to get out of line, then the reintroduction of the weekly report should tell you where things are going wrong.

Management Style

The establishment of standards and systems must be backed up by your own management style. This not only includes your manners with your staff, but also your response to situations that require action.

Always remember that, as the owner, it is up to you to instruct your staff in the way their jobs are to be done. You're controlling your staff; your own behavior sets an example.

Presumably, your long-range goal of success means that your behavior will reflect the standards and systems you have created. That, in turn, will influence your staff's behavior when following your standards and systems. For example, if, when you're helping to plate dinners, you use excessive portions, your staff will too when you're not around.

Remember to be consistent. Too often, owners vary their actions, and that does not offer a clear picture to employees. Such inconsistency confuses the staff and tends to water down whatever control you've created.

Staff Training

Setting an example for staff to follow in standards and systems is not enough. You must first train your staff in these areas before you can expect your example to be followed.

Initially, you must create a complete training program for each job category in your operation: manager, chef, cooks, dishwashers, janitors, servers, bartenders, hostesses, busboys, etc.

You must write out their job descriptions for them, telling them what they will be expected to do. They must be instructed in product knowledge (what you sell and how). They'll have to be taught your standards for products as well as your systems for handling and producing these products, and your systems for sales cash-control and remittances for the staff that serves customers.

Although a lengthy process, it must be done if you are to expect a professional staff. And every time a new person is hired, you'll have to do it all over again.

Staff Monitoring

One of your most important tasks is to control your operations by continually observing the actions of all of your staff as they go about their daily tasks. You must judge their actions in light of your standards and systems, and correct them when necessary.

The object of this monitoring is to change or modify the staff's job performance, or to control each person's job activity, so that it is consistent with your standards and systems.

For example, if you observe a bartender mixing drinks without measuring the ingredients and fail to direct him to measure, then your bartender could assume that his work is acceptable. You have just missed an opportunity to apply a control to a job task that was not consistent with your standards and systems.

The effectiveness of your standards and systems depends on the continuous monitoring and correction of your staff. Staff that follow the standards and systems should receive a positive response and praise, but conversely, those staff members that do not follow the guidelines must be corrected, and may require retraining in the particular task.

Other Considerations

Some other reports and forms that you may want to consider are as follows:

1. Beverage inventory control form
2. Beverage requisition form
3. Spillage, spoilage, breakage report
4. Bin control form
5. Purchase order form
6. Labor cost report
7. Waiting list form
8. Staff schedule form
9. Shift change form
10. Sign in/out form
11. Vacation report
12. Server/cashier remittance report
13. Costed inventory reports
14. Payroll deduction authorization form
15. Purchase summary report
16. Equipment history report
17. Staff time cards
18. Kitchen/bar transfer report

In general, you must remember that at the heart of the control process are three basic steps.

Begin by establishing both your standards and systems for operations. Be as thorough as possible. These are the building blocks of control, and there must be a firm foundation to build on.

Measure performance in all areas from your own management style to your staff's training and monitoring. Adhere closely to those standards and systems. Don't deviate as your success will depend upon them. And finally, through your reporting, learn how to analyze information early. The variances between your potential and actual standards and systems will eat up your profits, so take action quickly to correct these areas.

13

PERSONNEL

One of the most important assets in your new restaurant will be your staff. That single point must be remembered at all times.

Consider that the staff you hire represents your restaurant to the public. They're the first and last people that your customers will meet. They sell your products, or waste them, or steal them from you. Their service may make or break you. Or even worse, they may try to rip off your customers, and everyone will hear about that!

Whatever they do, you are paying them for their actions. You expect them to follow the standards and systems you've created for them, and you'll use both training and monitoring to ensure that they do. But never forget that you must set an example they can follow.

So how do you begin? You might find it easier to look at your personnel needs as a series of seven stages, or steps, that should be followed *in order* from planning, right through to training.

Policy

This first step is one that will be very important to you as the owner of a new restaurant. The policies you set down before you open are the rules and regulations, the law, if you will, that your staff will have to live by. And they are also loaded with information that your staff will want to know. Consider some of the following areas:

SAMPLE #18
The Seven Steps to Organizing Personnel Needs

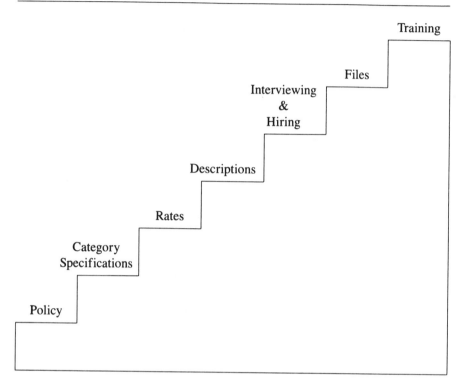

Probation Period
How long will your employees be on probation? Will you sit down with them at the end of this time and evaluate their performance?

Discipline and Dismissal
What constitutes a disciplinary situation? How will you discipline employees? How many such situations are grounds for dismissal? What constitutes grounds for immediate dismissal? Theft? Lateness? A no-show for a shift? An unclean uniform? Are you aware of standards laid down in the federal and state labor laws?

Staff Meals
Does your staff eat free when on duty? Or at half-price? Or what? Can they have anything they want? Or selected items only? Can

they drink alcohol on duty? Do they get any discount when they come in as customers? Are there some who'll have to pay and others who won't? Where can they eat? In the dining room? Or do you have a separate place for them?

Staff Breaks

Who gets a break? For how long? Do you pay them for that break? What are the labor laws concerning breaks? Where do they take their breaks? Who do they ask for a break, or do they just walk off the floor?

Staff Smoking

Are staff allowed to smoke at their work stations? In the dining room? On their breaks? Or not at all?

Schedules

When will the week's schedule be posted? Can they ask for specific time off? Do they just switch shifts with each other or must you okay it? What about vacations? How far in advance must they request vacations? What if they all want the same day or week off? How will you decide?

Staff as Customers

Can your staff stay after work as customers? Can they come in on days off? Must they keep to the front-of-the-house areas? Are they allowed to charge meals? Or drinks?

Uniforms

Will you have any? Do you supply them? To all or just some of the staff? Or does your staff buy them? What about cleaning? Repairs? Deposits? What about shoes? What colors and styles are acceptable? And nylons? Aprons? If employees wear their own clothes, what styles and colors are acceptable?

Cash Responsibility

Are the staff members who handle cash responsible? Do they make up shortages? How will you collect those monies? What about improperly verified credit-card vouchers?

Staff Areas

Can staff be in the back of the house when they're off duty? Where will their friends/spouses wait for them to finish after hours?

Payroll

When is payday? Do you pay extra for public holidays? What deductions might affect all or some staff? Will you cash their checks? How often do you review rates?

Tip Splits

Will you collect all or some portion of the tips? How will you distribute it among other staff members?

Staff Hygiene

Have you considered acceptable hair styles? Make-up? Jewelry? Their hands for cleanliness? Nail polish colors?

Category Specifications

Throughout your new restaurant, each position falls within one of the traditional job categories—from chef to sous-chef to line cooks, prep cooks, dishwashers, janitors, managers, assistant managers, floor supervisors, servers, bartenders, busboys, hostesses, and bar porters. And each of those categories will need just so many people to fill your needs. These category specifications are planned out according to the line chart in Chapter 4. You'll plan to fill each category to the maximum level needed to run your restaurant. But be forewarned about the experience factor. For example, at opening you may have to put eight servers on the floor to cover the dining room. But a month later, after they are experienced, only six or seven are really needed to handle the floor. So what do you do with those extra servers? You can partially get around this problem by using part-time staff right from the start. That way, you'll not be cutting down on your full-time staff. Natural attrition may also solve this problem.

Rates of Pay

Begin this third step by checking around in your community as to what rates are being paid for each job category. Your local restaurant and foodservice association office will supply you with a breakdown of these rates. Study them carefully, since it's your money you're looking at. Check around with other owners as to their rates. Remember that many of these rates will be based on experienced staff. But you'll be most interested in starting rates, taking into account minimum wage amounts.

As well as establishing your starting rates for each category, you should decide when the staff will be eligible for raises. This information should also be passed on to the staff, reminding them that raises will be based on performance and merit, not just on length of employment.

Job Descriptions

The fourth step is to take each job category and write a complete job description for it. This job description will also be handed out to all employees so they know just what is expected of them. It will clear up any misconceptions or excuses like "you didn't tell me I had to do that."

For example, here is a job description for a server in a full-table-service, licensed restaurant:

1. To serve every guest with courtesy and a smile.
2. To check in 15 minutes before each shift to receive cash register key, guest checks, section assignment, and daily special information.
3. To arrive each day in a clean, neat uniform and with personal appearance in accordance with policy.
4. To be fully knowledgeable on all menu items and prices.
5. To know proper garnishing of menu items and bar items.
6. To check each server station to see if it's fully stocked.
7. To check your section and see that every table is properly set.
8. To check the chairs, booths, and rug for dirt or crumbs.
9. To make sure coffee's hot and ready on each server station.
10. To inform your supervisor in case of customer complaints, equipment malfunctions, or poor housekeeping by cleaning staff.
11. To perform any other duties as may be requested (covers anything else you may forget).

Interviewing and Hiring

The fifth step uses all of the previous steps and is often the hardest. It involves the actual interviewing of everyone who applies for a job with you. But before you can interview, you have to know what you're looking for in each job category.

For each category, remember to list the four analysis points to use when interviewing. They are as follows:

1. Knowledge: What knowledge is needed to do this job?
2. Skills: What skills are needed to do this job?
3. Physical: What are the physical demands of the job?
4. Personal: What personal qualities are necessary for the job?

As an example, here's a job analysis for the cashier category.

1. Knowledge:
   (a) How to make change accurately
   (b) How to make up a cash report for each shift
   (c) How to record adjustments
   (d) How to handle credit-card vouchers, travelers' checks and government checks
   (e) How to handle customer complaints
   (f) How to service the cash register for tape or ribbons
2. Skills:
   (a) Basic math, English, reading, and writing
   (b) Skill and speed on a cash register
   (c) A courteous and friendly manner of speaking
3. Physical:
   (a) Ability to stand up for a long time
   (b) Ability to punch in number keys on cash register
4. Personal:
   (a) Responsible, fast, and efficient
   (b) Sociable and tactfully cooperative
   (c) Cheerful, but tough when necessary
   (d) Honest

Regardless of whether your applicants are walk-ins, come from employment agencies or schools, are referrals, or are responding to a newspaper ad, your next step is to have everyone fill out an application form.

The application form is used: (a) to gather all personal data you may need, (b) to show past work experience and educational levels, (c) to help you direct questions arising from the information given and general data required.

The application can, therefore, reduce the time you spend on each interview, while still giving you vital information in areas you would question. It can also aid in quickly eliminating candidates without the skills or experience you need.

Once the application is completed, it's your turn. Interview applicants in private—you're trying to get each candidate to open up to you, and that's impossible when surrounded by other candidates.

Ask questions that call for more than a "yes" or "no" answer. Don't ask a server candidate if they like being a server; instead ask them what they like/dislike about their job, and why?

Check their listed skills by asking them about their training for those skills. Or ask a technical question about those skills to test their knowledge and see if they really do have a particular skill.

Always refer to the past employment record and get them to explain why they left. This will give you some information as to how they perceived their old job and past employers.

Then tell them about what happens next: how long you'll be considering applications, when the candidates will be notified if they're hired, when the starting dates are, etc. These things are important to your applicants, so be honest with them.

Remember too, that you want the applicant to talk as much as possible. Listen well, and take notes on what is said and let them sell you on themselves.

After the interview is over, you should then check the references of every applicant who is a serious candidate. Simply call the listed employers and ask their opinion of the applicants' work habits, skills, performance, etc. This will give you a good idea of any problems in the candidates' past employment histories.

You now have all the information that can be gathered on each candidate. It is time to make your decision. Use your written notes to create a strength/weakness outline for each applicant. Both will be present, of course, for each position you have. Remember that each staff member is very important to your operation, so rate them on a scale from one to ten, according to how well you think the candidate can fill the requirements of the position.

You now have a list of their knowledge, skills, physical abilities, personal characteristics, references, strengths and weaknesses, and a risk-rating to help you decide.

Files

It is very important to set up personnel files for your restaurant. Purchase one of the pre-printed cardboard file-folders available. The covers have space to allow you to insert all personal information on each employee such as: name, address, Social Security number, the person to notify in case of emergency, any medical plan, and income tax ratings, etc. Space is also provided for your comments concerning promotions, tardiness, discipline, etc.

You will soon learn that the restaurant business, like all other businesses, generates a lot of paper. But these personnel files should not be forgotten; you'll refer to them regularly, and an updated, complete set of files is a necessary part of the smooth relations between you and your staff.

Training

The seventh and final step is the training of your newly hired staff. This training program is often assembled into a training manual for instruction to the staff, and a staff handout for them to study and refer to.

The general purpose of any training program is to turn these newly hired staff members into "professionals," regardless of their previous experience, and to improve the performance of each staff member.

The benefits of any training program are varied. They help your staff to earn a pay check and tips, satisfy your customers, and build your sales, which will lead to your new restaurant's success.

In any training program, regardless of your individual restaurant type, there are some basic areas to cover in depth. Generally they are as follows:

Product Knowledge—standards
Your staff must be knowledgeable about your complete menu, both food and beverage items. You must tell and show them your

standards for all items, from the receiving door to the customer's plate or glass. They must know what constitutes a perfect meal, in quality and portion quantity. They must know what plate or glass is to be used so they will be able to properly serve and sell the items on your menu to your customers.

Job Procedures—systems

This area, again to be fully developed and presented to the staff, will explain how to do each task in every job category. Although lengthy, these procedures will show the staff the correct way to follow the systems you created in Chapter 12. In order for your restaurant to run smoothly, everything must be listed, and taught to your staff, from how to cook a prime rib of beef, to how to greet and seat guests; from how to carry a trayful of drinks, to how to mix a drink.

Selling Aids

Because your servers will be the direct link to your customers, you must inform them about how you are going to enable them to sell.

Use your menu to show what is for sale, and what accompanies each meal. Teach them about your bar listings too—they're a great check-builder. What other things are available that may not be on the menus? Do you have blackboards with daily specials? Or placemats? Is there a childrens' menu? Or an after-theater menu? Show each one of the servers, and test them on their product knowledge.

Remember, to help your servers sell for you, you must fully develop these aids and systemize all of the procedures they will be using to sell.

Recipe File

This file is created for instruction of all production staff. Generally, the recipe file is composed of every menued or featured food and beverage item (*see* Chapter 12).

It lists ingredients and qualities and quantities to be used, and the procedure to be followed every time that item is produced. This ensures that the consistency of the menu item is constant in taste and quality.

Often these recipes are printed or typed on cards for easy reference by your kitchen or bartending staff. Many restaurants include a photo of the finished item so the staff will be consistent about plate arrangements as well.

As the owner, you'll not only want these recipes followed religiously for consistency of taste, but to ensure that the production staff are following the standards and systems set up to control your food and beverage costs.

Conclusion

Any new restaurant has problems in almost every area, and yours will be no different. One thing to remember is that your new restaurant will probably have few problems in attracting customers right off the bat.

The difficult thing is to please them that first time. If you lose them because they are not happy, it's very difficult to get those dissatisfied customers to come back again.

One of the best tactics to use in smoothing out those opening problems, is to organize dry runs.

This tactic involves providing a full-service meal to selected guests for free (or perhaps all monies might be donated to a charity).

Basically it's to give your staff the time to fine-tune your standards and systems. Begin by splitting your categories in half, wherever possible. The first dry run would be planned using one-half of the staff to come in to work and completely set up the restaurant for service. The second group then comes in as customers. They are seated, served, etc. After they have gone, the working half then closes up. Then reverse the two groups, and do the same again. Next, you might invite all of the tradesmen in, or your suppliers, or your family and friends, or local merchants, or business people, or all of them for staggered meal periods.

They'll act as "guinea pigs" for your systems. Problems will surface quickly and you'll be able to adapt before you have paying guests. And the experience your staff gains will outweigh the costs of such dry runs.

Once you are open, you're not finished by any means. Just because you've trained all your staff, don't think it's over. Training employees never stops. The staff are constantly leaving one position for another, and you'll have to train your new employees as well as your opening staff were trained. You'll also have to motivate them to help your new restaurant to succeed.

14

SUPPLIERS

As a new restaurateur preparing to open your business, you must realize the way in which suppliers view you. Certainly, the sales staff look on you as potential new business, the life-blood of successful sales people, but every supply company has a killjoy, and his title is usually credit manager.

To the credit manager, you are another potential risk in an industry with a high mortality rate. So as far as he is concerned you will have to prove you are worthy before he allows you the privilege of credit.

The procedure that many suppliers are now adopting is that your first order, which is always the largest, will be delivered C.O.D. Then, depending on the supplier, he may give you terms ranging from 10 to 30 days. Sometimes a supplier may not offer you credit for the first month or two, until he sees how your business is progressing.

Your progress can easily be determined by the volume of product that are ordering, or by the local salesperson dropping into your location, at what should be a peak time for business, to see how busy you really are.

Service versus Price

Service
As an operator in the service industry, you have deadlines to meet daily. When a customer comes through the door of your restaurant, the meal that he is expecting has to be available. This can

only be achieved if you have ordered the product and your supplier has delivered it.

Consequently, service by the suppliers you use must be high on your list of requirements, and equally important is the availability of the products you need. T.O.S.'s (temporarily out of stocks) can't be served to the customer. So service and availability are the hallmarks of a good supplier. These requirements can be established prior to opening, by talking to other restaurants serviced by the supplier, and will very quickly be confirmed once you are open.

Price

The price you pay for the goods you receive is also very important, but low price and poor service will most definitely cost you more money in the long run. If various items are constantly T.O.S., then you'll be running to the corner store or local supermarket and paying far more than you should.

You must also be wary of the supplier who comes in with the lowest prices initially and then gradually raises them over the next few weeks or months. Many new operators are so concerned with the day-to-day running of their restaurant that they fail to notice prices creeping up, especially if they are not taking time to phone other suppliers to compare prices. Remember, if you can save $100 per week because of good buying practices, that money is direct profit because your menu prices are often fixed for a 3-to-6 month period, and product price increases cannot always be passed on to the customer immediately.

The Sales Representative

As we mentioned earlier in this chapter, the life-blood of selling is new business, and to the supplier's sales staff, you are new business. Although most reputable companies give the sales staff strict guidelines to follow when selling, not all sales persons follow these instructions to the letter. Some of the questions you should ask are:

1. What is the minimum dollar or case delivery?
2. What credit terms can be arranged or can you expect, once you are established?
3. Does the company deliver every day in your area and, if not, what are the delivery days?

4. What time of the day can you expect delivery?
5. What is the cutoff time for ordering to receive delivery the following day?
6. When an item is T.O.S., does the supplier call you to let you know, allowing you to substitute, or does the company just deliver without the item, or substitute at the same price?
7. Are the delivery personnel unionized, and has the supplier experienced many labor disputes?

Once you have discussed all these points with your sales representative, don't be afraid to confirm the details with the company's sales manager and credit manager.

Other Services

Suppliers can provide many other services, such as:

1. Product information
2. Product-manufacturers' recommendations on cooking, storing, and serving ideas
3. New products on the market
4. Equipment related to the service of their products

The last item can be a great initial cost saving to the new restaurateur. For example, some coffee companies will provide coffee machines at no up-front cost to you, as long as you only use their product in the machine. However, there may be an up-charge in the cost of the product you purchase, i.e., 10¢ per lb. extra for the coffee.

Many other types of companies also offer this kind of service, such as ice-cream suppliers, carbonated-soft-drink suppliers, milk suppliers, etc. But it should be remembered that the supplier will only offer this service if he feels that your volume of purchases from his company is high enough to justify the capital expense his company will incur. In other words, nobody is going to give you something for nothing.

Receiving

Checking off the suppliers' delivery slips against what you have received is a task that any member of the staff should be able to complete. But knowing if the product is acceptable is something that only an experienced person can decide, especially when dealing with produce, meats, and fish products. It is therefore essential that you try to schedule all deliveries at a time when they can be received and checked properly, and that any unacceptable items can be noted on the delivery slip and returned immediately. Products delivered during a busy lunch period, not only fail to get checked properly, but often do not get put into storage until after the lunch rush is over. For perishable goods, this can not only be costly, but very dangerous.

Good ordering and receiving practices are as important for your restaurant's success as any other control.

15

ADVERTISING AND MARKETING

Introduction to Advertising

Before you can develop a marketing or advertising plan, you have to understand and determine three areas:

1. What advertising is
2. Why it is necessary to advertise
3. Who you are trying to reach with your advertising

What is Advertising?
Advertising can take the form of anything from the sign that hangs in front of, or on your building, to a full 60-second advertisement on national television, as well as 1,001 things in between. It can include daily specials, coupons, newspaper advertising and local radio spots—in fact, anything to let the public know you are there.

Why Advertise?
Many restaurants will advertise when they open, or when they have a special event or deal to offer. But what advertising really does is let the public know you are there and constantly remind them of that fact.

Who Should Your Advertising Reach?
In past chapters, we have discussed your customer profile, the type of persons who will frequent your restaurant. If you have accurately determined your customer profile, then you should know who you are trying to reach with your advertising. What remains to be determined is how to reach them.

Dangling the Carrot

When determining what your advertising approach should be, it is worth recalling the reason for opening your restaurant in the first place. Was it a great new concept? An original menu item? To fill a void in the market? Whatever the reason, this should be the basis for your initial advertising theme. If you're the only licensed pizza restaurant in town, let everyone know it.

Advertising on a Shoestring

Advertising doesn't have to be expensive. A television advertisement would certainly reach the greatest number of people, but the cost could never be justified in relation to the return for a single-restaurant operator. Your goal is to reach the largest number of people that fit your customer profile for the smallest amount of dollars.

Initial Advertising Ideas

There are certain strategies that can be used on a one-time basis when you first open up for business.

1. A personal visit by you to all the retailers and businesses in your immediate area, perhaps accompanied by a coupon, should be your first step. If they like what you have to offer, they will most definitely recommend your establishment to their employees and customers.
2. Prepare a news release about your new restaurant opening, together with a picture, if possible, and take it to your local newspaper. Remember to tell them that you are considering advertising in their paper once your operation has become established. These papers are always looking for stories with local interest, and may even send a photographer down, once you are open.
3. Having posters prepared by local graphic artists is another fairly inexpensive form of advertising. These posters can be placed (with permission) at other local high-traffic areas your customers would frequent, such as bowling alleys, ice rinks, movie theaters, shopping centers, clubs, local retailers, etc.

Keeping the Customer Satisfied

All of the previous ideas are certainly not expensive, and should let the public know you are there. But when it comes right down to it, there are many ways to get a customer to come into your restaurant, *once.* Getting them to come back a second, third, and fourth time will not depend on outside advertising, but on what you do inside your restaurant. Good food, friendly service, will be the most effective advertising your business will ever have. It doesn't cost anything, but it does take hard work and good management.

Getting to the top is the second-hardest thing in any business; the hardest thing is staying there.

Marketing

Marketing is often used as another word for advertising, but for the purposes of the new or existing restaurant we are going to show how you can market to the fullest the goods and services you have to offer. If these principles are adopted prior to opening your new restaurant, then you will have far greater successes than if you try to make changes after you are off-and-running.

There are five basic ways for any foodservice operation to increase or maximize sales:

1. Increasing selling prices
2. Outside promotions
3. In-House promotions
4. Extending your hours of operation
5. Increasing the average guest check

Increasing Selling Prices

This is often the first method that operators think of, but it should be remembered that these increases have to be over-and-above the normal price increases that would take place to offset higher food and labor costs.

The costs of this strategy are relatively small and may only include the reprinting of menus. Although you will achieve lower food and beverage percentages, you must allow for customer resistance, and may find that your sales do not actually increase. In fact, you may be pricing your operation out of its market position.

Outside Promotions

Outside promotions can be achieved in two ways: by use of the media, (television, radio, newspapers) to put your name in front of the buying public, or by the distribution of coupons, flyers, and discount certificates within your primary trading area to encourage local traffic.

Both these forms of advertising are geared to immediately increase your customer counts. The cost of buying media time or space, and the production and distribution of a coupon/flyer promotion, can be fairly easily established.

But don't forget to calculate the hidden costs of this strategy, including the value of the redeemable coupon, time spent in administration, acceptance of the program, and the possibility of coupon abuse.

This method can achieve the result of turning the short-term increase of new customers into long-term repeat business, with resulting higher sales.

In-House Promotional Events

They can be great fun for customers and staff alike, promoting a specific food item (Lobster Feast) or the creation of a theme event (Hawaiian Night). Although this is an in-house promotion, it is often necessary to advertise locally to maximize results.

How to calculate the supply and demand of the special food item, and the staffing requirements for that event, is often the main concern of the operator.

The costs of this program would include local advertising, in-house signage, decor, and novelties, but don't forget the higher food cost on the feature item. Of course, you hope to generate increased sales for the promotional period, with the possibility of repeat business from new customers.

As well, these events generate a high morale among your staff and recreate enthusiasm among your regular customers.

Extending Your Hours of Operation

This is often overlooked as a method of increasing sales. Although this can be very successful, you have to establish a need within your market.

All the fixed costs of the operation remain the same, and good management ensures that food and variable costs remain at the same percentage levels. All that you are risking by this method is additional labor dollars, unless there is a need for menu expansion.

Increasing the Average Guest Check

This is the easiest and cheapest method of increasing sales in any type of operation, and the one that's most often overlooked.

There are three principles that must be followed if this method is to succeed.

Show and Sell

This principle involves showing the customer food and beverage items that are for sale. This will create impulse-buying of items by the customer through visual displays.

Examples of this method would be the use of a well-presented salad bar, strategically placed to be highly visible, or the use of a dessert-and-pastry trolley moving through the restaurant.

One of the newest show-and-sell methods is the wine trolley. Here, the operator provides a mobile trolley with a knowledgeable staff member to market his wines throughout the operation. The guest is offered a sample of his or her choice, resulting in increased customer awareness of wines and a higher guest check.

Other show-and-sell techniques include an appealing back-bar display for your stand-up bar patrons, walking specialty cocktails through the dining room to pique your customers' curiosity, or preparation of food items in front of the customer. Many food-service outlets feature full-color pictures on the menu, or on menu-boards, of certain food items.

Tell and Sell.

This principle involves staff participation and well-presented signage. The use of feature boards is growing in many restaurant operations, but blackboard signs must be both uncluttered and artistic to gain appeal and instant item-recognition.

The strategic placing of these boards is also very important. Not only customers entering, but also seated customers must be able to see your feature items.

Table tent cards can be another great selling tool, but they should be professionally prepared. Remember to change them constantly as there is nothing less appealing than a tattered or stained tent card.

Staff telling-and-selling is the cheapest method, but for some operators, the hardest to carry out. It requires total involvement of management and staff to (a) inform the customer in an appealing way as to what your specials are, and (b) to increase the guest check and to build the bottom line by featuring specials that have a lower food cost.

These specials can be items purchased on a special deal, or ones that are seasonally available at a lower cost.

Selling up.

The normal approach by waiting-staff is to ask the customer for his or her order and place it at the bar and kitchen. The selling-up principle involves getting your staff to consider themselves as salespersons, and to treat the menu as their sales catalogue. Then, their whole approach to service will change.

Your staff, after taking the initial order, should then start selling-up by asking, or reminding each customer of the additional items that complement the order: "Would you like mushrooms with your steak, Sir?"; "Will you be going to the salad bar for starters?"; "Would you care for a liqueur with your after-dinner coffee?"

Try adding different features to your sales catalogue. For example, the choice of a larger-size drink at a relatively small price increase gives your salesperson the opportunity to sell-up in size, thereby increasing the guest check and building the bottom line.

Cost of implementation of these principles is very little, except for any additional aids that may be required, such as trolley, blackboard, or tent cards. The main thing that is required is time—time in preparation, training, and motivating your "salespersons".

Training sessions should be planned to reinforce their knowledge of the sales catalogue and the new selling techniques (tell and sell and selling-up) that they are going to be using. You may be surprised how much more involved your staff become in the operation, especially if you support this program with sales contests for the top seller (by item, period of time, or sales).

The results of these principles benefit both owner and staff, and are easily and immediately measurable.

1. Higher sales, with the same customer count
2. Lower labor percentage

3. Increased bottom line
4. Increased staff morale
5. A higher guest-check averages and higher tips for staff
6. Lower staff turnover

The best result of all, could be a higher repeat-business from your customers who enjoy the happy environment that you have created with your professional sales team.

16

"A DAY IN THE LIFE"

Throughout the past fifteen chapters, we have attempted to instruct and guide you in each step necessary to planning your new restaurant.

By now you're close to opening. You're working overtime on the final stages: training your staff; getting final inspections by the regulatory agencies for permits and licenses; using your sales projections to estimate your purchases of opening inventories; setting up your dry runs and grand opening.

And really, you've only just begun. From opening day, the workload on you, the owner, increases. And with that workload comes the responsibility of operating your restaurant smoothly and profitably—a responsibility that entails making judgments accurately and immediately when a situation requiring action arises. The need for and the ability to exercise "situational control," is mandatory. Such situations arise daily, hourly even, and must be dealt with on the spot. Now, none of us are perfect; we often make mistakes. But the onus is on you, as the owner, to judge these situations and apply control by making a decision immediately. Right or wrong, you must decide and follow through.

Like the home-plate umpire in baseball, you must call "balls and strikes," every time a pitch is thrown. As well, you must also judge "safe or out" whenever a runner slides home, and live with these decisions after the fact. You must know both teams playing, their personalities and the little tricks by which they bend the rules. You must also be aware of the strengths and weaknesses of the umpires under you, your key personnel, if you will, who'll help to control the game. And now that your restaurant is open, the responsibility for control is up to you.

What kinds of situations can arise? Well, as a hypothetical example, let's take a look at just thirty minutes in a typical "Day in the Life of a Restaurateur."

The time is 11:00 A.M., on a Friday, in Jim's licensed restaurant. There's a knock on the restaurant office door. "Yes? Who is it?"

"It's your number-one hostess, boss. Say, you look terrible! Can I get you a coffee?"

"Huh? . . . oh yes, black please, Lori. I was here until 2:30 A.M. last night. The damn cash wouldn't balance."

"Okay. One black coffee coming up. By the way, the toilets are blocked in the ladies' room again."

"Just what I needed," Jim said. "Now where did I put that snake for unblocking the toilets? Is was around here somewhere." Lori entered again as Jim seached around for the plumber's helper.

"Here's that coffee, boss. And Nancy just called; she's sick again."

"That's the third time this month. Boy, she gets sick a lot lately. And only one hour before opening. It figures. Do me a favor, Lori, and call someone else in to cover for her?"

"Sure. Anyone special?"

"No. Anyone will do. Wait it's Friday isn't it? Lunch will be busy. Betty's too inexperienced, Cathy gets too flustered when 200 people walk in. Who does that leave? Laura? Sure, Try Laura."

"She'll never get a babysitter this late," Lori informed him. Jim sat again, and stared at his staff schedule. "Right," he said, "I forgot. Okay, then try Elaine or Sandy or . . ." Another knock on the door interrupted him.

"Excuse me, Mr. Smith, what's the special for lunch today?"

"Oh, hi, Rich . . . special . . . lunch? What are you talking about? It should be ready by now. See the chef. Now, Lori, try . . ."

"Uh, the chef isn't in yet," Richard interrupted.

"What! Where the hell is he? I just can't understand that man. Why would he . . ."

"Elaine or Sandy, right?" Lori said.

"Oh, yes. One or the other," replied Jim trying to collect his thoughts. "Okay, Lori, try Sandy first. If she can't come in, then we'll pay for Elaine's cabfare. Just get someone for lunch, please. Now scoot! Okay now you, Rich. No chef and no special, right?"

The prep cook shifted his weight from foot to foot and started to apologize for his chef. "He'll probably show up soon."

"Yes," Jim said, "and probably hungover again. Is anything thawed out?"

"Not really, and there's no lettuce. The order hasn't come yet."

"Of course, it never rains but it pours. Here's $10. Send the dishwasher to Loblaws and tell him to buy all the lettuce, then dive into the freezer for me and yank out two, no three cases of those portioned steaks. Drop them into a full sink of running cold water, remember, like I showed you before, and they'll thaw out quickly. Okay?"

"Right, Mr. Smith, the lettuce and steaks."

Jim leaned back for a moment, and then turned to the safe. In the middle of taking out his float to set up his cashier's till, he heard yet another knock on his office door. "Boss, the draft beer isn't working again."

"What's up, Frank? Did you hook up the new kegs?"

"Oh, yes, but just one of them, that's all, honest."

"Frank, how many times must I tell you, you don't hook up a keg the day it's delivered. It's been bounced around too much. So take it off the line, then bleed the foam out of the lines and let it sit. It should be okay by opening. And Frank, don't let this happen again!"

"Sorry. Oh, and my cash register is out of tape and the box in the storeroom is empty," said Frank apologetically.

"Terrific! Listen, call Bernie down the street for me. He has the same cash register and tape sizes. See if he'll send up a few rolls for now by cab, C.O.D. I haven't got time to go and get it."

"If he can't, boss, I'll go get some," replied Frank as he left the office. Jim went back to his counting but only for a minute.

"Boss, Elaine's on her way in. Sandy wasn't home, so I'll need cab money."

"Sure, Lori. Here's $5; that ought to cover it."

"And there's two guys out front to see you. One's a salesman, I think."

"Get his card, and tell him not now. Anytime after 3:30 or so is fine. Who's the other?"

"I think it's the guy who had his coat stolen out of the coat-check last week."

Jim started going through his file tray in front of him. "Oh, yes, now where did I put that insurance-claim form? Have him wait, and I'll bring it out to him. Get him a coffee or something for now, will you?" Jim kept searching, reminding himself that he'd have to file this stuff sooner or later.

"Boss?"

"Sometimes . . . Frank," said Jim threateningly.

"A Mr. Owens called while you were busy and I took a message."

"Owens? My accountant?" Jim questioned.

"I guess so. Anyway, he said he needed last April's costed inventory, invoices, and reports. Said his girl lost the copies or something."

"Did he say by when, as if I didn't know?"

"He's sending his girl over right now."

"Of course. How's the beer? And tapes?"

"Tapes are on their way. The beer? I had to throw about twenty pitchers down the drain," apologized Frank.

"Oh well . . . drain? Damn! I almost forgot the ladies' toilets," Jim said. "Excuse me, I have to go be a plumber!" And he began looking for the plumber's helper once again.

As we've just seen, the normal workload of a restaurateur is often complicated by other situations. Everything seems to happen at once, and at the worst possible time.

Let's take a look at some of the qualities our restaurateur showed when dealing with these situations.

1. He was up until 2:30 A.M. balancing the cash so as to have an accurate picture of sales.
2. He'll unclog his own toilets and save money on an emergency plumbing call.
3. He knows his staff, i.e., who's been sick.
4. He knows who's capable of filling in on shifts, and who's not and why.
5. He's able to handle a crisis in food production by knowing what's on hand.

6. He knows his beer products and handling.
7. He knows how to correct mistakes in equipment use.
8. He knows where to borrow products quickly.
9. He knows how to schedule his time correctly.
10. He knows how to be a diplomat when dealing with customers.
11. He knows how to organize his records, even if he sometimes can't find the time to do so.
12. And he knows how to organize his own time for salesmen.

Once your restaurant is open and successful, it is very tempting to sit back and bask in the enjoyment of a profitable business. But you must remember that the life cycle of any successful restaurant is, at best, short. You must constantly move with the times and trends in order to keep your operation vibrant and interesting to your clientele.

The successful operator, who stays at the top for many years, is not necessarily physically harder than anyone else, but is mentally reviewing and planning ways his restaurant can better serve the needs of the buying public.

Those entrepreneurs who have been successful enough to turn a single operation into a national chain are the ones who have never been satisfied with their accomplishments. They are always striving to do better and improve upon what they have achieved.

APPENDIX:
SOURCES OF INFORMATION

State/Local Restaurant Associations

ALABAMA
Alabama Restaurant and Food
  Service Association
2100 Data Drive, Suite 207
Birmingham, Alabama 35244
205/988-9880

ALASKA
Alaska Cabaret, Hotel and
  Restaurant Association
P.O. Box 10-4839
Anchorage, Alaska 99510
907/272-8133

ARIZONA
Arizona Restaurant Association
2701 North 16th St. #221
Phoenix, Arizona 85006
602/258-3256

Southern Arizona Restaurant
  Association
Tucson Chamber of Commerce
  Building
465 W. St. Mary's Road, Suite 300
Tucson, Arizona 85705
602/791-9106

ARKANSAS
Arkansas Hospitality Association
603 Pulaski Street
P.O. Box 1556
Little Rock, Arkansas 72203
501/376-2323

CALIFORNIA
California Restaurant Association
3435 Wilshire Blvd.
Suite 2606
Los Angeles, California 90010
213/384-1200 or 800/252-0444

California Restaurant Association
1600 K Street, Suite 100
Sacramento, California 95614
916/447-5793

Golden Gate Restaurant Association
291 Geary Street, Suite 600
San Francisco, California 94102
415/781-5348

COLORADO
Colorado-Wyoming Restaurant
  Association
899 Logan Street
Denver, Colorado 80203
303/830-2972

CONNECTICUT
Connecticut Restaurant Association
19 Wallingford Road
Cheshire, Connecticut 06410
203/271-2151

DELAWARE
Delaware Restaurant Association
325 East Main Street
Newark, Delaware 19714-7838
302/366-8565

DISTRICT OF COLUMBIA
Restaurant Association of
  Metropolitan Washington, Inc.
7926 Jones Branch Drive
Suite 530
McLean, Virginia 22102-3390
703/356-1315

FLORIDA
Florida Restaurant Association
2441 Hollywood Blvd.
Hollywood, Florida 33020
305/921-6300

GEORGIA
Georgia Hospitality and Travel
  Association
600 West Peachtree Street, Suite 1500
Atlanta, Georgia 30308
404/873-4482

HAWAII
Hawaii Restaurant Association
1188 Bishop St., Suite 2611
Honolulu, Hawaii 96813
808/536-9105

IDAHO
Idaho Restaurant and Beverage
  Association
P.O. Box 1594
Boise, Idaho 83701
208/345-9830

ILLINOIS
Illinois Restaurant Association
250 West Ontario
Chicago, Illinois 60610
312/787-4000

INDIANA
Indiana Restaurant Association
2120 North Meridian Street
Indianapolis, Indiana 46202
317/924-5106

IOWA
Iowa Restaurant and Beverage
  Association
415 Shops Building
Des Moines, Iowa 50309
515/282-8304

KANSAS
Kansas Restaurant Association
359 South Hydraulic
Wichita, Kansas 67211
316/267-8383

KENTUCKY
Kentucky Restaurant Association
422 Executive Park
Louisville, Kentucky 40207
502/896-0464

LOUISIANA
Louisiana Restaurant Association
2800 Veterans Blvd., Suite 160
Metairie, Louisiana 70002
504/831-7788

MAINE
Maine Restaurant Association
5 Wade St.
P.O. Box 5060
Augusta, Maine 04330-0552
207/623-2178

MARYLAND
Restaurant Association of
  Maryland, Inc.
7113 Ambassador Road
Baltimore, Maryland 21207
301/298-0011

MASSACHUSETTS
Massachusetts Restaurant
  Association
11 Lakeside Office Park
607 North Avenue
Wakefield, Massachusetts 01880
617/245-8411

MICHIGAN
Michigan Restaurant Association
690 E. Maple, Suite 205
Birmingham, Michigan 48011
313/645-9770

MINNESOTA
Minnesota Restaurant and
  Foodservice Association
871 Jefferson Avenue
St. Paul, Minnesota 55102
612/222-7401

MISSISSIPPI
Mississippi Restaurant Association
P.O. Box 16395
4506 Office Park Drive
Jackson, Mississippi 39206
601/982-4281

MISSOURI
Missouri Restaurant Association
P.O. Box 10277
4140A Broadway
Kansas City, Missouri 64111
816/753-5222

Missouri Restaurant Association—
  St. Louis Area
2385 Hampton Avenue, Suite 111
St. Louis, Missouri 63139
314/645-1990

MONTANA
Montana Restaurant Association
P.O. Box 1193
Great Falls, Montana 59403
406/761-6370

NEBRASKA
Nebraska Restaurant Association
5625 "O" Street Building
Lincoln, Nebraska 68510
402/483-2241

NEVADA
Nevada Restaurant Association
3017 West Charleston Blvd., Suite 50
Las Vegas, Nevada 89102
702/878-2313

NEW HAMPSHIRE
New Hampshire Hospitality
  Association
P.O. Box 1175
15 Pleasant Street #14
Concord, New Hampshire 03301
603/228-9585

NEW JERSEY
New Jersey Restaurant Association
853 Kearny Avenue
Kearny, New Jersey 07032
201/997-8800

NEW MEXICO
New Mexico Restaurant Association
2130 San Mateo Blvd., NE; Suite C
Albuquerque, New Mexico 87110
505/268-2474

NEW YORK
New York State Restaurant
Association
505 Eighth Avenue, 7th floor
New York, New York 10018
212/714-1330

New York State Restaurant
Association
7916 Oswego Road
Liverpool, New York 13088
315/652-6555

NORTH CAROLINA
North Carolina Restaurant
Association
P.O. Box 6528
Raleigh, North Carolina 27628
919/782-5022

NORTH DAKOTA
North Dakota Hospitality
Association
P.O. Box 428
Bismarck, North Dakota 58502
701/223-3313

OHIO
Ohio State Restaurant Association
490 City Park Avenue, Suite 200
Columbus, Ohio 43215
614/228-0522

Northeastern Ohio Restaurant
Association
155 Main St.
Chardon, Ohio 44024
216/881-5232

Northwestern Ohio Restaurant
Association
1955 S. Reynolds Road, Suite 5
Toledo, Ohio 43614
419/389-0501

OKLAHOMA
Oklahoma Restaurant Association
3800 North Portland
Oklahoma City, Oklahoma 73112
405/942-8181

OREGON
Oregon Restaurant and Hospitality
Association
3724 N.E. Broadway
Portland, Oregon 97232
503/249-0974

Oregon Restaurant and Beverage
Association
2573 12th Street, SE
Salem, Oregon 97302
503/399-1272

PENNSYLVANIA
Pennsylvania Restaurant
Association
501 N. Front St.
Harrisburg, Pennsylvania 17101-
1011
717/232-4433

Western Pennsylvania Restaurant and
Hotel Association
470 The Landmarks Building
1 Station Square
Pittsburgh, Pennsylvania 15219
412/281-6388

Philadelphia-Delaware Valley
Restaurant Association
1411 Walnut St., Suite 200
Philadelphia, Pennsylvania 19102
215/567-6528

RHODE ISLAND
Rhode Island Hospitality
Association
P.O. Box 7415
Cumberland, Rhode Island 02864
401/334-3180

SOUTH CAROLINA
South Carolina Restaurant
Association
510 Barringer Building
1338 Main Street
Columbia, South Carolina 29201
803/254-3906

SOUTH DAKOTA
South Dakota Restaurant
  Association
805 1/2 S. Main Avenue
Sioux Falls, South Dakota 57101
605/332-1971

TENNESSEE
Tennessee Restaurant Association
P.O. Box 1029
229 Court Square
Franklin, Tennessee 37064
615/790-2703

TEXAS
Texas Restaurant Association
P.O. Box 1429
Austin, Texas 78767
512/444-6543

UTAH
Utah Restaurant Association
141 Haven Avenue, Suite 2
Salt Lake City, Utah 84115
801/487-4821

VERMONT
Vermont Lodging and Restaurant
  Association
97 State Street
Montpelier, Vermont 05602
802/229-0062

VIRGINIA
Virginia Restaurant Association
2101 Libbie Avenue
Richmond, Virginia 23230
804/288-3065

WASHINGTON
Restaurant Association of the State
  of Washington, Inc.
722 Securities Building
Seattle, Washington 98101
206/682-6174

WEST VIRGINIA
West Virginia Restaurant
  Association
P.O. Box 2391
Charlestown, West Virginia 25328
304/342-6511

WISCONSIN
Wisconsin Restaurant Association
122 West Washington Avenue
Madison, Wisconsin 53703
608/251-3663

Foodservice
Operator
Associations

AMERICAN CULINARY FEDERATION
Box 3466
1010 Bartolla Road
St. Augustine FL 32084
904/824-4468
professional chefs

AMERICAN HOTEL & MOTEL ASSN.
1200 New York Avenue N.W.
Suite 600
Washington, D.C. 20005
202/289-3100

AMERICAN INSTITUTIONAL
FOODSERVICE ASSN.
PO Box 155
Midvale UT 84047
801/268-3000
association for foodservice
executives/managers in
non-commercial operations.

CHEFS de CUISINE ASSN. OF
AMERICA
830 Eighth Avenue
New York NY 10019
212/262-0404
professional chefs

FOODSERVICE & LODGING
INSTITUTE
1919 Pennsylvania Ave. NW,
Suite 504
Washington DC 20006
202/659-9060
foodservice chains

INTL. FOODSERVICE EXECUTIVES
ASSN.
111 E. Wacker Dr.
Chicago IL 60601
312/644-6610
executives in all types of foodservice

INTL. SOCIETY OF HOTEL & MOTEL
MGMT. COMPANIES
c/o American Hotel & Motel Assn.
1200 New York Avenue N.W.
Suite 600
Washington DC 20005
202/289-3100

NATL. ASSN. OF CONCESSIONAIRES
35 E. Wacker Dr.
Chicago IL 60601
312/236-3858
food/beverage concession operations
in recreational-type
establishments; popcorn
processors and merchandisers;
suppliers

NATL. RESTAURANT ASSN.
1200 17th Street N.W.
Washington DC 20036
202/331-5900
foodservice operators from all
segments but primarily
restaurants; suppliers

SOCIETY FOR FOODSERVICE
MANAGEMENT
304 W. Liberty St.
Louisville KY 40202
502/583-3783
serving business/industry segment,
including independent and
contract-managed foodservices;
suppliers

SOMMELIER SOCIETY OF AMERICA
561 Broadway
New York NY 10012
212/941-1375
wine importers, restaurant owners
and other professionals

Operator Associations Indirectly Involved in Foodservice

AIRPORT OPERATORS COUNCIL
INTL.
1220 19th Street N.W.
Washington DC 20036
202/293-8500

INTL. ASSN. OF AMUSEMENT PARKS
& ATTRACTIONS
4230 King St.
Alexandria VA 22302
703/671-5800
operators and suppliers

INTL. ASSN. OF AUDITORIUM
MANAGERS
500 N. Michigan Ave., Suite 1400
Chicago IL 60611
312/661-1700
managers of auditoriums, arenas,
exhibit halls and stadiums

INTL. FRANCHISE ASSN.
1350 New York Avenue N.W.
Suite 900
Washington DC 20009
202/628-8000
major foodservice/fast food
franchisors

NATL. ASSN. OF TRUCK STOP
OPERATORS
P.O. Box 1285
1199 N. Fairfax St.
Alexandria VA 22313
703/549-2100
large full-service truck stops and
suppliers

NATL. SKI AREAS ASSN.
P.O. Box 2883
20 Maple St.
Springfield MA 01101
413/781-4732

OUTDOOR AMUSEMENT BUSINESS
ASSN.
4600 W. 77th St.
Minneapolis MN 55435
612/831-4643
operators of road shows, carnivals

TRAVEL INDUSTRY ASSN.
1133 21st St. N.W.
2 Lafayette Center
Washington DC 20036
202/293-1433
Businesses, associations and other
groups involved in travel trade

Foodservice Manufacturer & Distribution Associations

AMERICAN INSTITUTE OF FOOD
DISTRIBUTION
28-12 Broadway
Fair Lawn NJ 07410
201/791-5570
market information service

CODE, INC.
Manor Oak Two, Suite 480
1910 Cochran Road
Pittsburgh PA 15220
412/343-3600
foodservice distribution organization

COMMERCIAL REFRIGERATOR
MANUFACTURERS ASSN.
1101 Connecticut Ave. NW,
Suite 700
Washington DC 20036
202/857-1145
manufacturers of commercial
refrigeration

FOOD EQUIPMENT
MANUFACTURERS ASSN.
111 E. Wacker Dr., Suite 600
Chicago IL 60601
312/644-6610
custom food equipment
manufacturers

FOODSERVICE EQUIPMENT
DISTRIBUTORS ASSN.
332 S. Michigan Ave.
Chicago IL 60604
312/427-9605
equipment and supplies
distributors/dealers

INTL. FOODSERVICE
  MANUFACTURERS ASSN.
321 N. Clark St.
Chicago IL 60610
312/644-8989
food, equipment and supplies;
  publishers, product promotion
  assns., advertising/PR agencies,
  consultants

NATL. FOOD BROKERS ASSN.
1010 Massachusetts Ave. NW
Washington DC 20001
202/789-2844
retail and foodservice food brokers

NATL. FOOD DISTRIBUTORS ASSN.
111 E. Wacker Dr.
Chicago IL 60601
312/644-6610
specialty food distributors

COMSOURCE
280 Interstate North Parkway
Atlanta GA 30339
800/366-7723 or 404/952-0871
distributor buying/marketing
  organization

NUGGET DISTRIBUTORS INC.
4226 Coronado Ave.
Stockton CA 95204
209/948-8122
purchasing co-op for distributors

Foodservice Promotion & Other Specialized Organizations

ALASKA CRAB INSTITUTE
c/o Evans-Kraft
190 Queen Anne Ave. N.
Seattle WA 98109 4924
206/285-2222

ALASKA KING CRAB MARKETING
  & QUALITY CONTROL BOARD
c/o Evans-Kraft
190 Queen Anne Ave. N.
Seattle WA 98109 4924
206/285-2222

ALMOND BOARD OF CALIFORNIA
P.O. Box 15920
Sacramento CA 95852
916/929-6506

AMERICAN ASSN. OF MEAT
  PROCESSORS
224 E. High St.
Elizabethtown PA 17022
717/367-1168

AMERICAN BAKERS ASSN.
1111 14th St. NW
Washington DC 20005
202/296-5800

AMERICAN DAIRY PRODUCTS
  INSTITUTE
130 N. Franklin St.
Chicago IL 60606
312/782-4888

AMERICAN EGG BOARD
1460 Renaissance Dr.
Park Ridge IL 60068
312/296-7044

AMERICAN FROZEN FOOD
  INSTITUTE
1764 Old Meadow Lane, Suite 350
McLean VA 22102
703/821-0770

AMERICAN GAS ASSN.
1515 Wilson Blvd.
Arlington VA 22209
703/841-8400

AMERICAN INSTITUTE OF BAKING
1213 Bakers Way
Manhattan KS 66502
913/537-4750

AMERICAN LAMB COUNCIL
c/o Evans-Kraft
190 Queen Anne Ave. N.
Seattle WA 98109 4924
206/285-2222

AMERICAN MEAT INSTITUTE
1700 N. Moore St.
Arlington VA 22209
703/841-2400

AMERICAN SOYBEAN ASSN.
777 Craig Rd.
St. Louis MO 63141
314/432-1600

AMERICAN SPICE TRADE ASSN.
c/o Lewis & Neale Inc.
928 Broadway
New York NY 10010
212/420-8808

BISCUIT & CRACKER MFRS. ASSN.
1400 L St. NW
Washington DC 20005
202/898-1636

BLUE DIAMOND GROWERS
1802 C St.
Sacramento CA 95814
916/442-0771

CALIFORNIA ARTICHOKE ADVISORY
BOARD
PO Box 747
Castroville CA 95012
408/633-4411

CALIFORNIA DRIED FIG ADVISORY
BOARD
3425 N. 1st St., Suite 109
Fresno CA 93726
209/224-3447

CALIFORNIA DRY BEAN ADVISORY
BOARD & BEANS OF THE WEST
531-D Alta Avenue
Dinuba CA 93618
209/591-4866

CALIFORNIA OLIVE COMMITTEE
1903 N. Vine, Suite 102
Fresno CA 93727
209/456-9096

CALIFORNIA PRUNE BOARD
World Trade Center, Room 103
San Francisco CA 94111
415/986-1452

CALIFORNIA RAISIN ADVISORY
BOARD
PO Box 5335
Fresno CA 93755
209/224-7010

CALIFORNIA STRAWBERRY
ADVISORY BOARD
PO Box 269
Watsonville CA 95077
408/724-1303

CALIFORNIA TABLE GRAPE
COMMISSION
PO Box 5498
Fresno CA 93755
209/224-4997

CALORIE CONTROL COUNCIL
5775 Peachtree-Dunwoody Rd.,
Suite 500D
Atlanta GA 30342
404/252-3663

CAREER APPAREL INSTITUTE
1156 Ave. of the Americas
New York NY 10036
212/869-0670

CLING PEACH ADVISORY
    BOARD
P.O. Box 7111
San Francisco CA 94120
415/541-0100

CONCORD GRAPE ASSN.
5775 Peachtree-Dunwoody Rd.,
Suite 500-D
Atlanta GA 30342
404/252-3663

DAIRY RESEARCH INC.
6300 N. River Rd.
Rosemont IL 60018
312/696-1870

DENMARK CHEESE ASSN.
570 Taxter Rd.
Elmsford NY 10523
914/592-5277

DISTILLED SPIRITS COUNCIL OF
    THE U.S.
1250 Eye St. NW, Suite 900
Washington DC 20005
202/628-3544

FLORIDA CELERY COMMITTEE
c/o Lewis & Neale, Inc.
928 Broadway
New York NY 10010
212/420-8808

FLORIDA CITRUS COMMISSION
c/o Ogilvy & Mather Public Relations
40 W. 57th St.
New York NY 10019
212/977-9400

FLORIDA FRUIT & VEGETABLE
    ASSN.
PO Box 140155
Orlando FL 32814-0155
407/894-1351

FLORIDA TOMATO COMMITTEE
c/o Lewis & Neale, Inc.
928 Broadway
New York NY 10010
212/420-8808

FOOD MARKETING INSTITUTE
1750 K St. NW
Washington DC 20006
202/452-8444

SOY PROTEIN COUNCIL
1255 23rd St. NW
Washington DC 20037
202/467-6610

FROZEN VEGETABLE COUNCIL
1764 Old Meadow Lane
McLean VA 22102
703/821-0770

GAS APPLIANCE MFRS. ASSN.
1901 N. Moore St.
Arlington VA 22209
703/525-9565

GLUTAMATE ASSN/UNITED STATES
5775 Peachtree-Dunwoody Rd.,
Suite 500D
Atlanta GA 30342
404/252-3663

GREEN OLIVE TRADE ASSN.
325 14th St.
Carlstadt NJ 07072
201/935-0233

GROCERY MFRS. OF AMERICA
1010 Wisconsin Ave. NW
Washington DC 20007
202/337-9400

IDAHO POTATO COMMISSION
PO Box 1068
Boise ID 83701
208/334-2350

INDA, ASSN. OF THE NONWOVEN
FABRICS INDUSTRY
1700 Broadway
New York NY 10019
212/582-8401

INTL. ICE CREAM ASSOC.
888 16th St. NW
Washington DC 20006
202/296-4250

INTL. ASSN. OF REFRIGERATED
WAREHOUSES
7315 Wisconsin Ave.
Bethesda MD 20814
301/652-5674

INTL. FOOD ADDITIVES COUNCIL
5775 Peachtree-Dunwoody Rd.,
Suite 500D
Atlanta GA 30342
404/252-3663

INTL. JELLY & PRESERVE ASSN.
5775 Peachtree-Dunwoody Rd.
Atlanta GA 30342
404/252-3663

MEAT IMPORTERS COUNCIL OF
AMERICA
1901 N. Moore St.
Arlington VA 22209
703/522-1910

MAINE POTATO BOARD
744 Main St., Room 1
Presque Isle ME 04769
207/769-2711

MAINE SARDINE COUNCIL
PO Box 337
Brewer ME 04412
207/989-2180

CHERRY MARKETING INSTITUTE
P.O. Box 30285
Lansing MI 48909
517/321-1231

NATL. ASSN. FOR THE SPECIALTY
FOOD TRADE
1270 Ave. of the Americas
New York NY 10020
212/586-7313

NATL. ASSN. OF BEVERAGE
IMPORTERS
1025 Vermont Ave. NW,
Suite 1205
Washington DC 20005
202/638-1617

NATL. ASSN. OF MARGARINE
MFRS.
1101 15th St. NW
Washington DC 20005
202/785-3232

NATL. BROILER COUNCIL
1155 15th St. NW
Washington DC 20005
202/296-2622

NATL. CHERRY GROWERS &
INDUSTRIES FOUNDATION
1105 NW 31st St.
Corvallis OR 97330
503/753-8508

NATL. CONFECTIONERS ASSN.
Ogilvy & Mather Public Relations
40 W. 57th St.
New York NY 10019
212/977-9400

NATL. FISHERIES INSTITUTE
2000 M St. NW
Washington DC 20036
202/296-5090

NATL. FOOD PROCESSORS ASSN.
1401 New York Ave. NW
Washington DC 20005
202/639-5900

NATL. FROZEN FOOD ASSN.
604 Derry Rd.
Hershey PA 17033
717/534-1601

NATL. ICE CREAM MIX ASSN.
5610 Crawfordsville Rd., Suite 1104
Indianapolis IN 46224
317/243-9342

NATL. KRAUT PACKERS ASSN.
108½ E. Main St.
St. Charles IL 60174
312/584-8950

NATL. LIVESTOCK & MEAT BOARD
444 N. Michigan Ave.
Chicago IL 60611
312/467-5520

NATL. PASTA ASSN.
1901 N. Moore St.
Arlington VA 22209
703/522-1910

NATL. MEAT CANNERS ASSN.
PO Box 3556
Washington DC 20007
703/841-2400

NATL. ONION ASSN.
1 Greeley National Plaza, Suite 510
Greeley CO 80631
303/353-5895

NATL. PEACH COUNCIL
3299 K St. NW
Washington DC 20007
202/965-7510

NATL. PEANUT COUNCIL
101 S. Pelton St.
Alexandria VA 22314
703/838-9500

NATL. PORK PRODUCERS COUNCIL
P.O. Box 10383
Des Moines IA 50306
515/223-2600

NATL. PREPARED FROZEN FOOD
ASSN.
99 W. Hawthorne Ave.
Valley Stream NY 11580
516/825-3000

NATL. SHRIMP PROCESSORS ASSN.
55 Park Place
Atlanta GA 30335
404/577-5100

NATL. SINGLE SERVICE FOOD
ASSN.
5775 Peachtree-Dunwoody Rd.,
Suite 500-D
Atlanta GA 30342
404/252-3663

NATL. SOFT DRINK ASSN.
1101 16th St. NW
Washington DC 20036
202/463-6732

NATL. TURKEY FEDERATION
11319 Sunset Hills Rd.
Reston VA 22090
703/435-7206

NEW JERSEY ASPARAGUS INDUSTRY
  COUNCIL
NJ Dept. of Agriculture CN-330
Trenton NJ 08625
609/292-8853

NORTH ATLANTIC SEAFOOD ASSN.
1220 Huron Rd.
Cleveland OH 44115
216/781-6400

PACIFIC COAST CANNED PEAR
  SERVICE
P.O. Box 7111
San Francisco CA 94120
415/541-0451

PACKAGING INSTITUTE, USA
20 Summer St.
Stamford CT 06901
203/325-9010

PEANUT BUTTER & NUT
  PROCESSORS ASSN.
9005 Congressional Court
Potomac MD 20854
301/365-4080

PICKLE PACKERS INTL.
108½ E. Main St.
St. Charles IL 60174
312/584-8950

PINEAPPLE GROWERS ASSN. OF
  HAWAII
P.O. Box 3829
Honolulu HI 96812
808/531-5395

POPCORN INSTITUTE
111 E. Wacker Dr.
Chicago IL 60601
312/644-6610

THE POTATO BOARD
1385 S. Colorado Blvd., Suite 512
Denver CO 80222
303/758-7783

POTATO CHIP/SNACK FOOD ASSN.
1711 King St.
Alexandria VA 22314
703/836-4500

POULTRY & EGG INSTITUTE OF
  AMERICA
1815 N. Lynn St., Suite 801
Arlington VA 22209
703/522-1363

PRIVATE LABEL MFRS. ASSN.
41 E. 42nd St.
New York NY 10017
212/972-3131

PROCESSED APPLES INSTITUTE
5775 Peachtree-Dunwoody Rd.,
  Suite 500D
Atlanta GA 30342
404/252-3663

PRODUCE MARKETING ASSN.
700 Barksdale Plaza
Newark NJ 19711
302/738-7100

QUALITY BAKERS OF AMERICA
  COOPERATIVE
70 Riverdale Ave.
Greenwich CT 06830
203/531-7100

RICE COUNCIL
P.O. Box 740123
Houston TX 77274
713/270-6699

SINGLE SERVICE INSTITUTE
1025 Connecticut Ave. NW,
Suite 1015
Washington DC 20036
202/347-0020

SOAP & DETERGENT ASSN.
475 Park Ave. S.
New York NY 10016
212/725-1262

SWITZERLAND CHEESE ASSN.
444 Madison Ave.
New York NY 10022
212/751-3690

TEA COUNCIL OF THE USA
230 Park Ave.
New York NY 10017
212/986-6998

TEXTILE RENTAL SERVICES ASSN.
1130 E. Hallandale Beach Blvd.
Hallandale FL 33009
305/457-7555

TUNA RESEARCH FOUNDATION
1101 17th St. NW
Washington DC 20036
202/857-0610

UNITED DAIRY INDUSTRY ASSN.
6300 N. River Rd.
Rosemont IL 60018
312/696-1860

UNITED FRESH FRUIT &
VEGETABLE ASSN.
727 N. Washington St.
Alexandria VA 22314
703/836-3410

UNITED STATES TROUT FARMERS
ASSN.
515 Rock St.
Little Rock AR 72202
501/372-3595

WASHINGTON STATE APPLE
COMMISSION
PO Box 18
Wenatchee WA 98801
509/662-2123

WESTERN GROWERS ASSN.
PO Box 2130
Newport Beach CA 92658
714/863-1000

WESTERN STATES MEAT ASSN.
1615 Broadway, Suite 1200
Oakland CA 94612
415/763-1533

INT'L. WILD RICE ASSN.
220½ NW 1st Ave.
Grand Rapids MN 55744
218/327-2229

WINE & SPIRITS WHOLESALERS
OF AMERICA
1023 15th St. NW
Washington, DC 20005
202/371-9792

WINE INSTITUTE
165 Post St.
San Francisco CA 94108
415/986-0878

Consultant, Research & Nutrition Associations

AMERICAN PUBLIC HEALTH ASSN.
1015 15th St. NW
Washington DC 20005
202/789-5600

AMERICAN SOCIETY FOR TESTING
& MATERIALS
1916 Race St.
Philadelphia PA 19103
215/299-5400

ASSN. OF FOOD & DRUG OFFICIALS
PO Box 3425
York PA 17402
717/757-2888

INTL. ASSN. OF MILK, FOOD &
ENVIRONMENTAL SANITARIANS
PO Box 701
Ames IA 50010
515/232-6699

INSTITUTE OF FOOD
TECHNOLOGISTS
221 N. LaSalle St.
Chicago IL 60601
312/782-8424

NATIONAL RESTAURANT ASSN.
EDUCATIONAL FOUNDATION
250 N. Wacker Dr., Suite 1400
Chicago IL 60606
312/715-1010

NATL. SANITATION FOUNDATION
3475 Plymouth Rd.
Ann Arbor MI 48106
313/769-8010

SOCIETY FOR NUTRITION
EDUCATION
1700 Broadway, Suite 300
Oakland CA 94612
415/444-7133

Trade Shows

The following is a list of annual trade shows in the United States. Contact your local restaurant association for further information.

AHA Convention & Trade Show (Arkansas Hospitality Association)
Annual Exposition & Culinary Show
Annual Maine Foodservice & Lodging Show
Annual Meeting & Convention
Annual New York Metro Foodservice Show
Annual Rocky Mountain Hospitality Convention & Educational Exposition
Annual Texas Restaurant Association Convention
ARK-LA-TEX Food & Equipment Exposition
Atlanta International Wine Festival
Carolina Foodservice Expo
Central Pennsylvania Food & Equipment Expo
East-South Regional Restaurant Convention & Exposition
Foodservice Expo
Greater Jacksonville Food & Equipment Show
Hospitality Showcase
International Foodservice Expo
International Hotel/Motel & Restaurant Show
Iowa Licensed Beverage Show
Iowa Restaurant Convention & Exposition
Louisiana Foodservice & Hospitality Exposition
Mid-Atlantic Regional Restaurant Mart
Midsouthwest Foodservice Show
Midway USA Regional Food Service Exposition
Midwest Regional Foodservice-Lodging Exposition
Michigan & Great Lakes Food Service Show
NAFEM (National Association of Food Equipment Manufacturers)
New Hampshire Hospitality Association Annual Meeting & Trade Show
New Jersey Foodservice Expo
New Mexico Hospitality Trade Show
New York State Restaurant Association's Foodservice Exposition
North Dakota Hospitality Show
Northeast Foodservice & Lodging Exposition & Conference
NRA Restaurant Hotel-Motel Show (National Restaurant Association)
ORA Annual Restaurant Convention & Exposition (Ohio)
ORA Soft Serv/Pizza Convention (Ohio)
Pacific Area Food & Beverage Exposition
Pacific Northwest Regional Restaurant Show & Educational Exposition
Philadelphia-Delaware Valley Restaurant & Hospitality Show
South Carolina Food Service & Educational Exposition
Southeastern Hospitality & Foodservice Show
South Florida Foodservice Expo
Tennessee Foodservice Exposition

Upper Midwest Hospitality Restaurant & Lodging Show
Virginia Foodservice Expo
Western Pennsylvania Restaurant & Hotel Assn. Trade Show
Western Restaurant Convention and Exposition
WRA Northwest Foodservice Trade Show (Wisconsin)
WRA/WIA Annual Convention and Trade Show (Wisconsin)

INDEX

INDEX